ALTERNACRAFTS

ALTERNACRAFTS

Jessica Vitkus

photographs by Brian Kennedy

illustrations by Elizabeth Lee

STC Craft/A Melanie Falick Book

Stewart, Tabori & Chang

New York

To my grandmother,
Theodora Vitkus Pazera,
whose hands are always busy making something beautiful.

Published in 2005 by
Stewart, Tabori & Chang
An imprint of Harry N. Abrams, Inc.

Edited by Melanie Falick

Book Design: Noël Claro
Production Director: Kim Tyner
Photostyling by Aaron Caramanis

Library of Congress Cataloging-in-Publication Data

Vitkus, Jessica.
Alternacrafts / by Jessica Vitkus.
p. cm.
Includes index.
ISBN 13: 978-1-58479-456-1
ISBN 10: 1-58479-456-9
1. Handicraft. 2. Recycling (Waste, etc.) I. Title.

TT157.V496 2006
745.5—dc22
2005013555

The text of this book was composed in Trade Gothic and Chalet

Printed in China

10 9 8 7 6 5 4 3 2

harry n. abrams, inc.
a subsidiary of La Martinière Groupe

115 West 18th Street
New York, NY 10011
www.hnabooks.com

CONTENTS

INTRODUCTION

In 1986, from my seat in a darkened movie theater, I watched Molly Ringwald stitch together a killer prom dress from ribbons and scraps. The movie was <u>Pretty in Pink</u>. I was ecstatic to see crafts taken out of the realm of the granny and put into the hands of the cool. (Well, Molly wasn't exactly cool in her fictional high school—James Spader was. And why wouldn't she hook up with Duckie?) But that movie brought home the message that making your own stuff is fun, cheap, and empowering.

And I have been crafting proudly ever since. Though my grandma taught me some tricks and gave me inspiration (she's a needlework genius), I've learned lots of techniques from books and magazines (thank you, Martha Stewart!). But no book or magazine has really spoken to me in terms of aesthetic or philosophy. So I thought I'd offer an alternative: <u>AlternaCrafts</u> (the cousin of alternative rock music). It's the book I wish I'd had the night before my prom.

The Ten Commandments of Crafting

By "commandments" of crafting, I mean "very strong suggestions." These are the crafting rules that I have figured out over the years, rules that I craft by, and rules that have helped keep crafting a practical pleasure. Whether you are new to crafting or have been at it for years, consider this advice.

I. Invest Yourself, Not Your Cash

A gift or home accessory or little fashion treat has so much more meaning if you make it yourself. Isn't that nicer than blowing a wad at the store? Wouldn't you rather have or give a one-time-only first edition with your creative mark built into it? Many of the *AlternaCrafts* offered here require very little time or money—you can make a laced-up T-shirt or a pierced-paper card in about ten minutes with stuff you already have. You can make an embroidered sachet or a bouquet of newspaper flowers in under an hour. But if you must choose between spending time or money, pick time. The investment will pay off better than any stock option. You'll make yourself proud, you'll have fun, you'll make someone happy.

II. Recycle, Recycle, Recycle

You know how much stuff we consume, we waste, we throw out. It's a giant shame. Well, you can undo the damage just a tiny bit by crafting with (ahem) pre-used materials. Turn old jeans into a bag, old sweaters into hats, old dress shirts into sachets, old T-shirts into a rug. Turn bottle caps into lockets instead of landfill. Mother Earth will thank you, and your friends will thank you when you give them cool gifts. And even if your final product is not made from old materials, you can use recycled stuff in the process. Start saving plastic take-out containers, yogurt cups, and glass jars. Use them to store buttons and sequins, or as a place to mix grout. As you start to craft from old materials, loved ones will start saving jeans, buttons, bottle caps, and jars for you. You get more free supplies. Your recycling program expands.

III. Leave Technology Behind and Use Your Hands

Crafts by their very nature are low-tech. Knitting and knotting and sewing and quilting are age-old art forms once done by firelight—often for practical more than decorative purposes. And while computers can now embroider and machines can cut paper, knit, and sew, we get enough machinery in daily life. Why not put that stuff aside? *AlternaCrafts* emphasizes the hand in handiwork. The only things you ever need to plug in are an iron or a woodburning tool. A sewing machine is helpful but super-optional.

IV. ... But Think Modern

This is not an old-fashioned craft book. Many of the techniques are old, but the designs and the uses are new. Next time you burn a CD for a friend, make a collage cover from found paper. Macramé a bracelet but use silvery washers and nuts from the hardware store as beads. Knot chopsticks into an elegant Zen place mat. Use pebbles or buttons to make an abstract mosaic that belongs in a modern art museum.

V. Open Your Eyes

Look for shapes and patterns and designs in your everyday life that excite you. How many times have you looked at a candy display wondering which chocolate bar to eat? Now look at that display as an array of packages—different materials, colors, text styles, pictures. Then buy your new favorite and make a wallet out of the wrapper. Keep your eyes open for cheap source materials—buttons, jeans, twigs, sweaters, old magazines. Look with crafty eyes at tag sales, thrift stores, junk drawers, attic boxes.

VI. Do Not Stay Within the Lines

Do not be afraid to be messy. Do not feel obligated to copy the *AlternaCrafts* example stitch-for-stitch, snip-for-snip. Experiment. If it helps to build your confidence, replicate a craft shown here to get the technique down, then try another, different version. There is not one right answer or one ideal result.

VII. Customize

Goods in stores are mass-produced for the masses. The crafter can customize. So, match the colors of your kitchen, embroider your best friend's initials, appliqué a self-portrait. If you know who the craft is for or where it's going to live, work that into the design.

VIII. Branch Out

If you've done a lot of work with fabric, try working with wood. If you are comfortable with paper projects, see how it feels to pound a hole in a metal bottle cap. Push yourself into new areas, new mediums (ok, media). You will probably bring fresh ideas along with you, you won't be bored, and you'll pick up some skills.

IX. Share the Wealth

If you find a craft you like (here or elsewhere), teach it to a friend. Do it in pairs or groups. Chat and exchange ideas. Time will fly by. (You can borrow each other's tools and supplies, too.)

X. Relax! Enjoy!

Don't stress if you don't finish on time or if you make a mistake. Deadlines are for school and the office. Mistakes are charming and human. If you aren't having fun or chilling out, put the project down and pick it up later. Who cares about the end product if you don't enjoy the process?

And if you still aren't inspired, go rent Pretty in Pink.

PROJECTS•TO•WEAR••PROJECTS•TO•WEAR

YOUR • LOOK *projects to wear*

RECYCLED•COZINESS

Hat from a sweater

In less than an hour, you can turn that sweater you never ever wear into a snuggly hat. It's the newest recycling program—minus the tax break.

Getting ready

Wool sweaters work best for this project because they are warm and the fibers are stretchy—so it's easier to get the size right. But the process will still work on a cotton or acrylic sweater. It's fine if your sweater has holes, as long as there is enough healthy stuff (about two 10-inch squares of hole-free area) near the bottom edge. The secret trick to this hat is this: The ribbed bottom edge of your sweater becomes the ribbed bottom edge of your hat.

How-to

Measure and cut two rectangles. Lay your sweater flat. Make sure the bottom edge of the sweater is a straight horizontal line but don't pull it taut. Measure, mark, and then cut out two rectangles about 9½ inches wide and 8½ inches tall, using the ribbed bottom of the sweater as one of the long sides. (These dimensions work for most adult women—make the rectangle wider for a big man and narrower for a

small child.) Remember, you will only be cutting out three sides; the bottom of your hat will be a nice, finished fourth side. Unless your sweater is really big, you will probably have to cut one rectangle from the front and one from the back. That's totally fine.

Cut six long strips from sleeves. Snip off one of the sweater sleeves. Then cut a straight line from the cuff to the armpit, making the tube into a flat piece. If there is a seam there, cut right alongside the seam, using it as a guide. If there is no seam, then follow a vertical row of knit stitches. Lay the sleeve flat with the cuff toward you. Cut a straight line across the top of the sleeve to even it out. Then, starting at the cuff, cut lengthwise to make strips about 1½ inches wide. Again, use the knit stitches as a guide for cutting straight—but if the strips don't come out perfectly straight, that's OK. You need six of them the same length. You will probably need to cut the second sleeve to get that many.

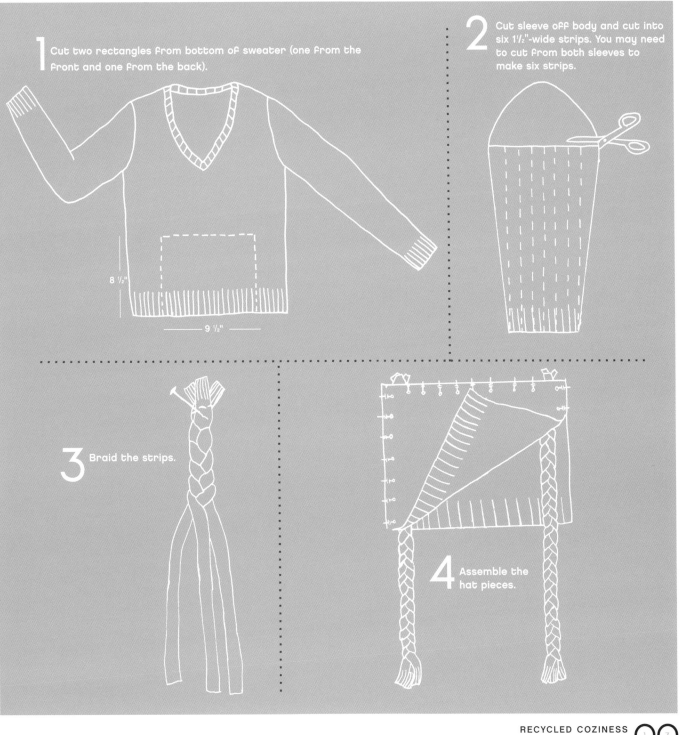

1 Cut two rectangles from bottom of sweater (one from the front and one from the back).

8 ½"

9 ½"

2 Cut sleeve off body and cut into six 1½"-wide strips. You may need to cut from both sleeves to make six strips.

3 Braid the strips.

4 Assemble the hat pieces.

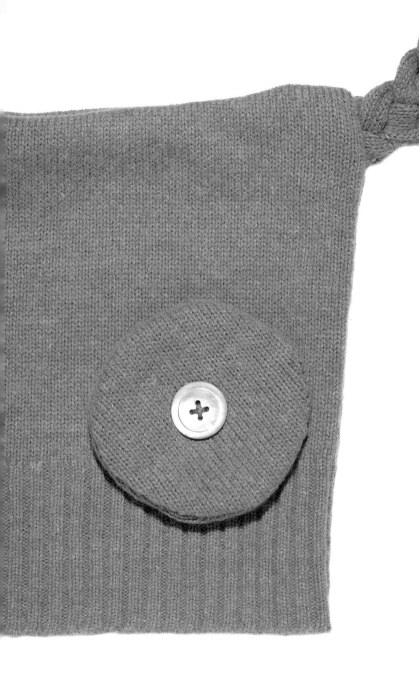

What to do with all that extra sweater? Well, you can make a decorative flower for your hat. Cut two circles about 5 inches in diameter from anywhere on the sweater (except the edges). Place them right sides together, and sew around the edges about $1/2$ inch in, but leave an opening to turn the circles right side out. (You are basically making a little round pillow without any stuffing.) Turn right side out and stitch the opening closed. Place a big button in the middle of the flower, then sew the button and the flower to the hat all at once. Or sew the flower (or two or three) onto another sweater like a brooch.

3 **Braid the strips.** Divide the strips into two groups of three. Make sure they are all turned the same way—right side up and cuff end toward you. Take one set, hold them together at the cuff, and sew them together about ½ inch or so from the edge of the cuff. Then pin that stitched end to a couch arm or rug and braid the strips. Stitch the three strips together at the other end. Repeat with the second set of strips.

4 **Assemble and pin in place.** Line up the two rectangles with the wrong sides together. The bottom of the sweater—now the bottom edge of the hat—is toward you. Sandwich the two braids between the rectangles with the raw ends of each braid (not the cuff ends) peeping out at each corner as shown on page 13. You can leave the braids as long as possible, or leave only 8-12 inches of braid dangling like ours.

5 **Sew together.** Make a running stitch along the three cut sides, about ½ inch in from the edge. When you get to the end, turn your work around and make another line of running stitches right next to the first one for strength. This should keep the knitting from unraveling.

6 **Turn right side out.** If you want, tie knots at the end of each braid for extra oomph.

FELT BETTER

Wool fibers have the unique ability to felt. That is, the little tiny threads unfurl and then tangle together tighter to form a bond. **If you have ever thrown a sweater into the wash by accident and it shrank, that was actually felting.** If your hat (of wool) came out too big or you are just feeling adventurous, try this experiment. Make a wool sweater-hat an inch or two bigger than indicated in the instructions. Then fill two big bowls with water—one very hot and one very cold. Dip the hat into the hot water with a little mild soap for 30 to 60 seconds, squeeze it out, then dip it into the cold water and rinse for 30 to 60 seconds. If not much happens the first time, repeat the wash-and-rinse procedure a couple more times. **Your hat should shrink and even thicken.** (It's hard to control how much felting will occur. It depends on what the sweater has been through already). If all goes well, your hat will be extra warm and sturdy. Felting shortcut: Put your hat and a little soap in a washer set for a hot wash and cold rinse. Periodically check on your hat to make sure it hasn't shrunk too much (if it has, give it to a kid!).

T-SHIRT•MAKEOVER•1

Lacing

T-shirts are the bread and butter of the casual wardrobe.

Comfy. Cute with jeans. Who here has fewer than ten of them?

But, like bread and butter, T-shirts can be boring.

This is the first of three ways to add flavor: a

no-sew lace-up seam where once there was none. This project

takes about five minutes (no joke). Do a whole bunch of tees at

a time and give them away to your friends. Lace and tie, and

suddenly you have modern epaulettes.

MATERIALS

T-SHIRT

2 SHOELACES (18" or longer)

TOOLS

HOLE PUNCH

Getting ready

First thing to do is gather up some T-shirts. This particular makeover works well with solid tees and tees that have writing or pics on the front.

How-to

1 **Plan out laces.** Lay the shirt out neatly on a table and finger-press flat along the shoulder, from the neck opening to the outer edge of the sleeve. This creates a line where the lacing will go.

2 **Punch holes.** Starting at the neck end of the crease, about an inch away from the neck opening, punch a hole through two layers of tee at once. As the shirt lies flat, the hole should be about ½ inch to 1 inch down from the shoulder crease. Punch another hole about 1 inch over from the first one. Repeat, moving down the sleeve until you reach the edge.

3 **Lace up.** When you open up the shoulder area you see pairs of holes for lacing. Starting at the neck end, lace up the edges much like you would lace a shoe. You can make neat Xs or skip around the holes for a messier look. Pull the shoelace as tight or loose as you want. Tie a knot or a bow at the sleeve edge.

4 **Repeat steps 1 through 3** on the other side of the shirt.

SIDE MAN

Use the same technique up the side of a tee. Find wild laces
in skate shops, sporting goods stores, or even record stores.
This technique naturally makes the shirt tighter and more
shapely. So you can rehab baggy ones and make 'em snug.

BOTTLE-CAP•LOCKETS

Metalworking meets scrapbooking

This project is a great way to recycle. Have a party just to generate bottle caps. Their ruffled edges make sweet little frames. Fill them with pictures and small treasures (seashells, buttons) to preserve forever. Since the lockets are so small, you can make a dozen or so in one sweep. Sure, they are not technically lockets that snap shut, but you can wear a portrait of a dear one near your heart just as ye olde locket-wearers did. Or dangle one from a belt loop (like ye olde folks *didn't*). Carry love (and art) with you wherever you go.

MATERIALS

10 TO 20 BOTTLE CAPS
(or larger metal lids)

EYE SCREWS

WHITE GLUE

PHOTOGRAPHS OF
FRIENDS AND FAMILY

3 TO 6 FEET BALL CHAIN
(available in hardware stores; if
you want to wear your locket on
ball chain, get the little end
fasteners too, or take one from
a key chain)

TINY DECORATIVE
DOODADS

EPOXY RESIN KIT (such as
Aristocrat Liquid Illusion,
available in craft stores)

ABOUT 2 FEET
RIBBON (or other decorative
cord) PER LOCKET

TOOLS

AWL

HAMMER

SQUARE OF SCRAP
WOOD, TO USE AS A
WORK SURFACE

PLIERS (optional)

QUARTER

PEN

SCISSORS

WIRE CUTTER

TOOTHPICKS

2 PLASTIC FILM
CANISTERS (or other small
disposable containers exactly
the same size)

RUBBER GLOVES

PINT-SIZED YOGURT
CONTAINER (or other
disposable plastic container)

WOODEN CHOPSTICK OR
POPSICLE STICK, FOR
STIRRING

PLASTIC FREEZER BAGS
(or any heavy plastic) AND
NEWSPAPER, TO
PROTECT WORK AREA

Getting ready

Find pictures that you like but are willing to sacrifice to the crafting gods. Not every locket works out, so don't grab that original print of grandma's wedding. Collect and wash bottle caps or, to make larger lockets, metal lids from juice bottles, baby food, jam, or mustard jars, or other sources.

As for decorative doodads, you can use sequins, beads, rhinestones, stickers, buttons — as many or as few of these as you want. Feel free to go beyond the store-bought. Baby teeth, tiny shells, pebbles, lace from an old shirt, small hardware bits, safety pins— these can all go into a locket.

On Craft Day, pick a work area near an open window—since the resin creates fumes—and spread out plastic bags and newspaper to protect your work surface.

How-to

1 **Make a hole in the bottle cap for the eye screw.** Choose bottle caps to make into lockets. Weed out caps that are too bent to use. Slight bends are okay—you can lay those caps down, ruffle facing up, and flatten them a bit by pushing down with your thumb. Once you have a good bottle cap, use the awl and hammer to make a hole for the eye screw. To do this, hold the bottle cap sideways on the wood scrap (ruffles parallel to the table). Place the tip of the awl in one of the troughs of the ruffle—about halfway to the bottle cap's edge—and tap it with the hammer

to make a hole (see photo at right). You can wiggle the awl in the hole or hammer it again if you need to make the hole a little bigger.

2 **Attach the eye screw.** This is the hardest (or the most annoying) part of the process. Patience and elbow grease are required. Hold the bottle cap in one hand and push the eye screw in with the other hand. Wiggle and twist the screw until the thread catches and it screws into the hole. (Holding the screw with pliers helps save your thumb.) If it won't go in, expand the hole a little with the awl. Once the screw is in place, dab white glue on the inside of the lid where the screw comes through—this will seal the hole so resin doesn't leak out later. Let dry.

3 **Cut out a portrait from your photo.** A quarter is the perfect template for a bottle-cap background. Center it over the portion of the photo you want to use, then trace around it with a pen and cut out along the tracing line. Place the cut-out circle into the bottle cap.

TIP

If the eye screw is very loose and wiggly in the hole, the hole is too big and resin will probably leak out (even with the glue seal). Either use a bigger eye screw or start over on a new bottle cap.

Steps 3 and 4: Cut out a portrait from your photo. Cut the chain to make a border.

4 **Make a chain border.** To make a chain border to hide the edge of the picture, use the wire cutter to cut about 3 inches of chain. Lay the chain into the bottle cap, nudging it with your finger or a toothpick until it sits on the edge of the picture. Snip off any extra chain, and push the ends into place so they touch and form a circle.

5 **Add decorations (if you want).** You might be happy to stop with a picture and chain border. That's fine, especially when it's an extra beautiful picture. If you want to add mementos and decorations, place a few in the bottle cap now. Keep in mind that things will move when you add the resin (which is part of the fun). Also remember that you can add more decorations later. Try not to obscure the loved one's portrait too much.

6 **Repeat steps 1 through 5.** Prepare up to 20 bottle caps. If this is your first batch ever, just make about 10 or so until you get a feel for working with the resin. You can always make more later.

7 **Prepare the resin mix.** Your resin kit should contain two bottles of liquid. One is resin, and the other is hardener. The kit might also have a mixing bowl or tray and a stirring tool (but those are less crucial since you have your empty yogurt cup and chopstick). Instead of mixing all the liquid at once, it's better to make smaller batches. Then you can save the rest for another day. Take your two film canisters and mark them R and H for "resin" and "hardener." They are now measuring tools, and if you use them for another batch later you need to be consistent about what you put in them. Put on the gloves and make sure you are working in a well-ventilated area. Carefully fill the R canister to the top with resin. Fill the H canister to the top with hardener. Pour them both into the yogurt container. Stir with the chopstick according to the kit's directions—usually agitating nonstop for about 2 minutes.

8 **Pour the resin.** Lay the bottle caps out on top of plastic freezer bags in a flat, level, and well-ventilated work area. Take the container of resin mix and squash the edge to form a spout (if it's flexible enough). Carefully pour a small amount of resin into the bottle caps—half of what you think it will take. Let the resin spread out, then decide if you want to pour in more. Do not fill the bottle caps to the top— too full means spills. Besides, it's interesting if pebbles and buttons peek out of the resin's surface.

9 **Adjust and add decorations.** This is the fun part. Take a toothpick and poke the beads, shells, and whatnot so they sit where you like. Add

BEYOND THE PORTRAIT

Sure, faces are nice, but you can fill your locket with any image you want. Make a locket homage to your favorite road sign or building. Don't just look at the faces in your photos, look at the skies and trees. Cut those—or any interesting images or textures— into little circles. Then you can let the objects in your bottle cap take center stage. **Who cares if the picture gets covered up?** Have fun with the collage part of the project. Expand your idea of things that can go inside— basically, anything that will fit. Colorful matchstick heads, paper clips, dried lentils, metal washers, or bits of ribbon can all fill your little lid masterwork. If you want to add text, keep in mind that paper soaks up resin and becomes sheer. Newspaper or magazine pages are very thin and text from the other side shows through. Magazine or catalog covers work better. Cut out words that have nothing much on the back. Some inks will dissolve in the resin, so keep that risk in mind. Arrange objects and words within the circle. Use the depth of the lid or cap to your advantage. Let words sit atop buttons or metal nuts. **Think in layers.**

Step 8: Pour resin over collage.

Skip steps 1 and 2 (which will save on time, tools, and thumb aches) and leave your bottle caps unpierced and unscrewed. Glue a round magnet onto the back and display your masterpiece on the fridge so you can admire it daily.

light decorations like sequins to the top and let them float there for a nice depth-of-field effect. If your work surface is not level, you'll notice that things drift to one side. Check for this over the first couple of hours, while the resin is still liquid. If necessary, shift the locket so it's sitting flat. Later you should check for lint and dirt that might have blown by and stuck to the surface. Gently wipe it off with your fingertip. Let the lockets dry for 24 hours or more (humidity will slow down drying). If a little resin leaks or sticks to the caps, you can just peel the caps off the plastic.

10 Add ribbons and chains. When the resin is completely dry, turn your lockets into jewelry. Run ribbons or pieces of leather or ball chain through the eye screws and wear on a belt loop or around your neck. You can also use (or give them) as key chains.

SMALL MESH CH_____E   LIGHT BROWN #405

Vogue **NYLON**

_____ _____ STYLES

15¢

HAIR NET

WITH

E L A S T I C

INVISI-MESH ● RESIST-RUN PROCESS

Joey Heatherton

SPARK

MILK
CaT LiTTer
SoyCrisps
manGOES
SelTzer

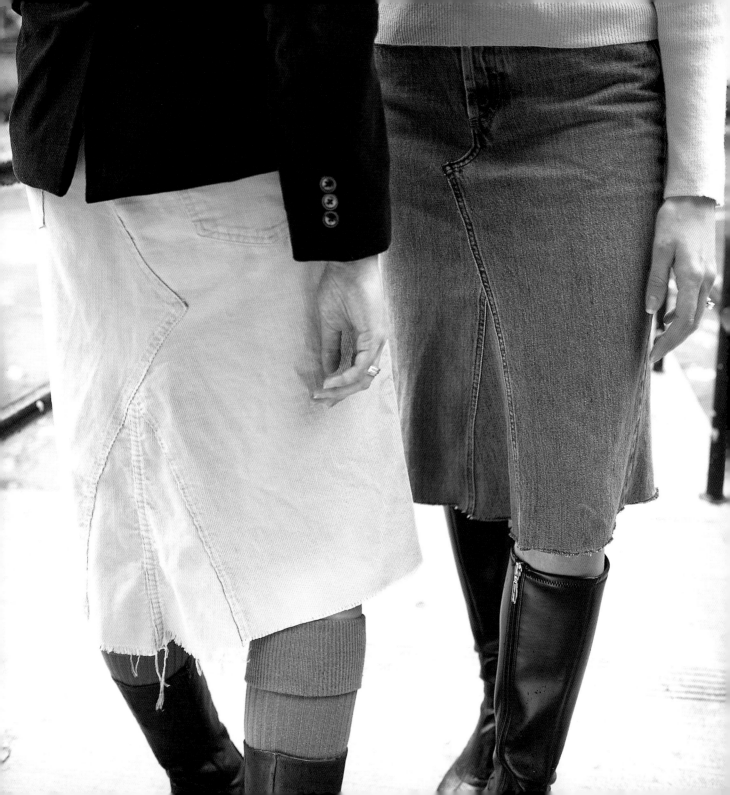

SKANTS

Skirt from pants

Take old jeans, cords, or army pants that you never wear any-more and convert them into a skirt. **The secret is in the pinning—**shape the butt exactly the way you want it. Who needs to hem? Just cut the bottom off to mini or maxi length. Takes a few hours if you sew by hand—minutes if you have a sewing machine—but **provides days upon days of high fashion.**

Steps 3-5: Pin, choose
length, and add a panel of
denim to front and back.

Getting ready

Try on any pants you are thinking of making into skants. Make sure you like the way they fit up top, because that's staying the same. If you are sewing by hand, settle in for a longer crafting session and consider sewing with bright embroidery floss. The handstitching then becomes a bohemian-style bonus.

How-to

1. **Open inseam.** Starting at an inner ankle, undo the inseam using scissors or a seam ripper. Be sure to cut the thread only—not the fabric. Open the seam all the way up the leg, across the crotch, and down the other leg until you finish at the opposite inner ankle. Most jeans have two rows of stitching, which take a little more work to rip out.

2. **Open front and back vertical seams.** There is a short seam that goes from the bottom of the zipper to the crotch of the pants. Undo that. Then turn the pants over and, starting at the crotch, rip out part of the vertical seam in the back, starting at the bottom and working upwards. Stop about halfway past the back pocket.

3. **Pin in place (while skirt is off).** The four fabric panels that made up the pants are going to overlap in two places—the front and the back. On the pants front, you'll see that the right panel—the one that makes up the front of the zipper fly—lies in front of the left panel. Pin it into place as shown at right so you create the front of the skirt with an opening in the shape of an upside-down V. On the back of the pants, look at the vertical seam. Take the panel that is already in front, and make it overlap the other one to form a skirt. Pin it into place. You are basically doing the same pinning job you did in the front, only this time you have to allow for the shape of your butt.

4. **Try on skirt and cut to desired length.** At this stage, it helps to have another person on hand, but it's doable on your own with a good full-length mirror. Be careful as you put on the pinned

HUSTLE AND BUSTLE

Instead of cutting the hemline even all around, **let it be longer in the back— which looks like a mini- train or bustle.** Or let it swoop down longer on one side—like an exotic flamenco dancer. If you don't like it, you can cut it again later.

skirt. When deciding how long you want it to be, err on the long side—you can always cut it shorter later. Either have your helper cut the hemline while you are wearing the skirt, or mark the length you want with a pin, take it off, and cut. If you want to leave the skirt full-length, that's fine, but you'll need to find some other fabric to fill in the upside-down V in front.

5 **Pin in fabric panels.** Take the skirt off, if you haven't already. Using the excess fabric you just cut off the bottom, pin a piece into each upside-down V opening. Make sure there is at least an inch of overlap. Cut fabric panel to correct length.

6 **Try on for final fitting.** This is the most important step because you are about to commit to the new shape. Try on the skirt and take time to fuss with the pinning so it lies flat in the front and hugs your butt in the back.

7 **Sew new seams.** You can do this by hand, making little running stitches on top of the flaps about ¼ inch in, or use a sewing machine. If you have the patience, make two rows of stitches where the old rows were—one very close to the edge, another about ½ inch from the edge.

8 **Trim excess.** Turn the skirt inside out and cut away the extra fabric that you just sewed into the V. Leave about ½ inch all around.

TROUBLESHOOTING

The biggest trouble spot is the top of the butt seam in the back—the place where the old seam meets the new one. It wants to buckle and pucker. Use extra pins to get it just right. You might even need to rip the old seam out farther and repin. But don't make yourself crazy. If the material is cotton, it will sort of shrink and mold into shape with future wearing and washing.

T-SHIRT•MAKEOVER•2

Mock smock

A series of little pin tucks creates the suggestion of smocking.

(Remember those smocked dresses you wore as a little girl?) In a

trice, you can give a flat, old T-shirt this

interesting light-and-shadowy texture.

TOOLS

SCISSORS

RULER

PENCIL OR TAILOR'S CHALK

HAND-SEWING NEEDLE

MATERIALS

T-SHIRT

MATCHING THREAD

Step 1: Turn shirt inside out and mark spots for tucks with Xs.

Getting ready

Raid your T-shirt pile for plain, solid-colored tees—those work well. But you can also try making tucks above, below, or right on top of a beloved image.

How-to

1 **Mark spots for tucks.** Turn the T-shirt inside out. Measure about 2 inches down from the front center of the neck. Mark a small X with the pencil (use tailor's chalk—or even a sliver of white soap—if the shirt is dark). Hold a ruler horizontally, just under the X you made. Mark another X 2 inches to the right of that center one, mark another X 4 inches to the right of the center one. Repeat on the left so you end up with a horizontal row of five little Xs—all 2 inches apart. Two inches below that row, make another horizontal row of Xs, each 2 inches apart—but this time there are only four marks, staggered so they fall in

Step 2: To create pin tucks,
work a stitch perpendicular
to the "pleat."

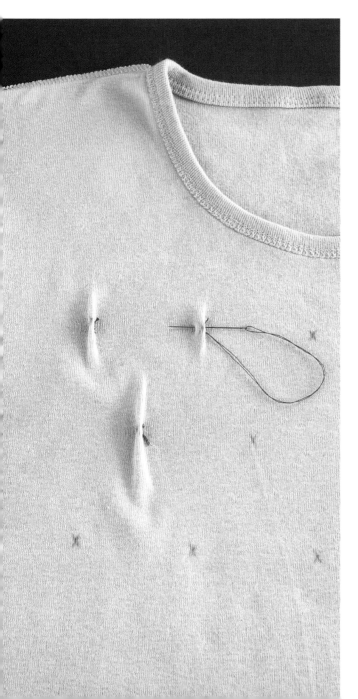

between the marks in the first row (see diagram at left). Two inches below the second row, make a row of five Xs just like the first row. In the end, you should have three rows of marks, as shown.

2 **Sew tucks.** Still working on the inside of the shirt, pinch the fabric to form a little vertical pleat with an X smack in the middle of it. The vertical line of the pleat should cut right through the center of the X. Sew a stitch about ¼ inch deep, perpendicular to the pleat edge, as shown in the photo at left. Bring the needle and thread through the pleat three or four times and then knot the thread. Pinch and stitch all the other Xs the same way.

3 **Turn the T-shirt right side out.**

SMOCK IT TO ME
Smocking was invented
by the Anglo-Saxons
many centuries ago. It
was (and still is) a
practical way to make a
garment warmer and
snugger where you need
it, like at the wrists
and chest.

CHAIN-MAIL • KNIT • CUFF

Instant wrist-wear

Feel as tough as a gladiator without all the nasty battle scars.

This cuff is so easy you can make it in a

couple of hours—even if the only thing you've ever

knit before is your brow. Make two in a metallic color and play

Wonder Woman.

MATERIALS

LIGHTWEIGHT METALLIC YARN (such as Lurex Shimmer by Rowan; one 104-yard/25-gram ball should yield at least 5 cuffs)

TOOLS

1 PAIR SIZE 6 KNITTING NEEDLES

RULER

SCISSORS

YARN NEEDLE

BETTER•THAN PROZAC

Research has shown that blood pressure and heart rate go down while knitting.

Getting ready

If you have never knit a stitch before and you have a knitter in your life, you might want to raid her (or his!) knitting basket for some scrap yarn. Make a practice swatch with any plain wool—it's stretchy and forgiving and less slippery than the metallic yarn. But if you just got back from the store and you only have the yarn for this project, that's fine.

You might also want to find a knitting tote bag. Knitting is a highly portable craft—you can knit on a plane or a car trip, while waiting at a doctor's office, or while chatting with a friend. So pop your supplies into a small cloth bag (one that the needles won't poke through) and get in the habit of taking it with you. It's a habit that might last a lifetime.

The other wonderful thing about knitting—it's very soothing. The small repetitive movements calm the nerves and focus scattered thoughts without taxing the IQ. It's really a form of meditation that also gives you cool stuff to wear. Can't beat that.

SCARF, ANYONE?

To get a rock star scarf as skinny as Iggy Pop himself, cast on 18 stitches and knit, knit, knit until you think it's long enough. To change colors or just start a new skein of yarn, knit to the end of the row and let the loose end dangle. Start a new row with new yarn, leaving 5 inches or so of tail to dangle, and knit across the row. To finish, tie the two dangling ends together, then weave them into the knitting with a yarn needle or crochet hook. Trim off the last inch or so of yarn, if necessary.

Step 5: Sew long edges to create a cylinder.

How-to

Note: If this is your first knitting project, turn to page 44 to learn all the techniques you need for this project.

1. **Cast on 25 stitches,** leaving a tail of about 3 inches when you make the starting slipknot. For a newbie, casting on can be the hardest part of knitting, and it's not very hard. There are many methods for doing this. My favorite (shown on page 44) uses two needles, which essentially knit the first stitches into place. Do the first few stitches slowly and carefully; your patience will pay off.

2. **Knit until piece is 6 inches long.** Guess what? The knit stitch is a very close cousin of the casting on stitch. Keep knitting rows until the piece measures about 6 inches. When measuring your work, lay it flat but don't stretch it out—that would be cheating.

3. **Check yarn location.** When you are done with your last row, your working yarn and your tail yarn should be on the same edge of the piece, not at diagonal opposite corners. If they aren't, just knit one more row.

4. **Bind off,** leaving an 18-inch tail of yarn attached to the knitted fabric. This step is easy and satisfying.

5. **Sew edges to form a cylinder.** Now you have a rectangle of knitting with two tails, one short and one long, at opposite corners. Thread the longer tail into the yarn needle. Hold the rectangle so it forms a cylinder, with the cast-on edge touching the bound-off edge. Sew the seam as shown at left, catching a stitch from each side. When you get to the end of the seam, tie the two tails together in a square knot and cut off the ends. (Normally knitters weave the ends into the work, but this metallic yarn is best just cut.)

HOW • TO • KNIT

Cast On

a

b

c

d

e

Bind Off

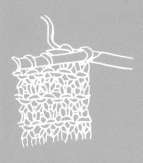

a

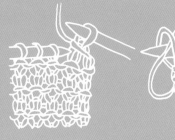

b

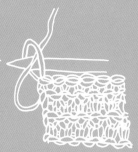

c

Knit Stitch

NOTE TO LEFTIES: Knitting uses the right hand and left hand almost equally, so there's no need to reverse these instructions. The process is a bit awkward for everyone at the beginning, but becomes more graceful with repetition.

Cast On

a. Make a slipknot, leaving a tail of about 3 inches, and slide the loop onto one of the needles.

b. Hold the needle with the slipknot in your left hand, keeping the slipknot near the needle tip. Insert the right needle into the loop on the left needle, going in front-to-back, so that you form an X with the needle tips as shown.

c. While your left hand holds the left needle (middle, ring, and pinky fingers curl around it), the left thumb and forefinger temporarily hold the right needle. So now your left hand is supporting both the needles, which frees up your right hand to do the work. Use your right hand to take the working yarn (the yarn that leads back to the ball, not the tail) and bring it under the right needle and between the crossed needles in a back-to-front motion.

d. Use your right hand to bring the right needle toward you, pulling the piece of working yarn you just laid there through the stitch on the left needle.

e. Now you have two loops: the old one on your left needle and a new one on your right needle. With your left hand, bring the left needle toward you and insert the tip into the new loop that's on the right needle, going in from bottom to top. Let the right needle slide out, slide the stitches down past the tapered part of the knitting needle, and pull the working yarn slightly to prevent loose loops. Repeat steps b through e until you have 25 stitches on the left needle.

Knit Stitch

This stitch follows the same steps as casting on through step d.

a. Hold the needle with all the cast-on stitches in your left hand. Hold the empty needle in your right hand.

b. With the extra yarn in back of the needles, insert the right needle into the first stitch on the left needle, going in front to back, just like you did for casting on.

c. Hold the right needle with your left thumb and forefinger. Use your right hand to bring the working yarn under the right needle and between the crossed needles in a back-to-front motion.

d. Use your right hand to bring the right needle toward you, pulling the piece of working yarn you just laid there through the stitch.

Here's where knitting differs from casting on:

As before, you have two loops—the old one on your left needle and a new one on your right needle. This time you simply slide the left needle out of the new loop and keep your new stitch on the right needle. (See illustration at left.) Repeat steps until all the stitches from the left needle are gone and the right needle holds a fresh row of knitting. Put the full needle in your left hand and the empty needle in your right hand and make another row just the way you made that one.

Bind Off

a. Knit 2 stitches. Insert the tip of the left needle into the first stitch you knit on the right needle as shown.

b. Lift the first knit stitch over the second knit stitch and off the needle. Knit the next stitch. Repeat bind-off steps a and b until there is just one loop left on the right needle.

c. Cut the working yarn, leaving about 18 inches of tail. Thread this new tail through the remaining loop and pull until it forms a knot.

JEAN-IUS•BAG

Purse made from jeans

If you have any jeans that don't fit or (worse) you succumbed

to the cropped bootcut jeans sale that seemed like a good

deal at the time, no worries. Make a bag that will be useful

(all the pockets still serve as pockets) and stylish.

Stylish because you customize to your heart's pleasure. Do it with or without a sewing machine.

All for pennies.

Steps 1 and 2: Measure
from top of the fly to the
crotch seam to establish
the height of your bag.
Draw a horizontal line all
the way around, then cut.

MATERIALS

OLD JEANS (or corduroys or
army pants)

THREAD IN A MATCHING
OR CONTRASTING COLOR

RIBBON, ROPE, OR
RICKRACK, FOR BELT

ANY OTHER
DECORATIONS YOU
WANT (sequins, buttons,
embroidery floss)

TOOLS

RULER

PEN OR TAILOR'S CHALK

SCISSORS

SEAM RIPPER (optional)

STRAIGHT PINS

SEWING MACHINE OR
HAND-SEWING NEEDLE

Getting ready

The era of low-cut jeans and stretch jeans has made
this project a little more challenging. Low-cut jeans
will still work, but they make a shallower bag. Stretch
jeans will work, but they are harder to sew—especially
with a machine. But it's all possible. The best
prospects are heavy, solid cotton (or cotton-blend)
pants, whose "waistline" hits above the hips.

How-to

1 **Measure and mark jeans.** Pants don't
always have the same amount of fabric in the front
and back. There's usually more room for your behind.
Since you don't want your bag to have a butt, measure
the distance from the very top of the fly to the crotch
seam. This will be the height of your raw, unsewn bag.
Say, for example, this height is 8 inches. Measure and
mark a dotted line that is 8 inches from the top of the
waistband on both the front and back of the jeans.

2 **Cut off pant legs.** Cut along the line you just
marked. Save the extra material for later.

Flatten jeans front. A body wearing jeans is three-dimensional, but the bag should lie flat. So there is a seam you must resew to make your bag more 2-D, less lumpy. Rip open the seam from the bottom of the zipper fly to the crotch (use the scissors or seam ripper to cut the thread only—not the fabric). That seam, which is only a couple of inches long, once formed a curve. Turn the jeans inside out and pin the opened seam back together so it makes a straight line down from the fly, and a flat front for the bag. Sew by hand or machine.

Sew bottom seam. With the jeans still inside out, line up the raw bottom edges and pin together. Sew across, about ½ inch in from the edge, either by hand or machine. Then sew across again, making this second seam just above and parallel to the first

Steps 3 and 4: With jeans inside out, open the curved seam that goes from the bottom of the zipper fly to the crotch, then resew in a straight line. Next, pin the bottom edges together and sew two lines of stitches to create a strong double seam.

one. You want your bag to be strong. This double seam has to take all the weight of whatever you're carrying.

5 **Cut strips for handles.** Cut a notch at the top of one of the remaining pant legs. Tear all the way down the pant leg. Use scissors to get through the bottom hem. Then measure 2 inches over from the first tear, make a notch, and tear again. You should end up with a strip 2 inches wide and about 20 inches long (if it's longer or shorter, that's okay). Cut another strip the same way, the same size.

6 **Sew on handles.** Take one strip, lay it right side up, and fold the bottom of the strip up 1 inch. (Iron the fold into place at high heat if you want.) This extra thickness at the bottom will give your strap extra holding power after you sew it on. Place the end with the folded-up tab on the inside of the bag's front waistband, with the tab side against the waistband, lining up the edge of the strap with the nearest belt loop. Pin the strap into place and sew a small rectangle with an X in the middle as shown. Repeat with the other end of the strap, placing it on the other side of the fly so it forms a mirror image. Repeat with the strap on rear side, making sure the back-strap ends line up with the front-strap ends.

7 **Decorate.** Thread a piece of ribbon, rope, or rickrack—depending on the look you want— through the belt loops and tie it in front. You can stop there or add buttons, rhinestones, embroidery, or sequins. When you want a new look, change the belt.

Step 6: Sew on handles.

GET • A • GRIP

Instead of making the straps from the pant legs, you can buy premade bag handles (see purple bag on page 46). Handles come in a huge variety of colors and materials (see your sewing store or www.mjtrim.com). Just sew them into place or tie each handle-end to the nearest belt loop with a ribbon.

T-SHIRT•MAKEOVER•3

Appliqué

Appliqué may be a big French word complete with its own accent, but it's just a fancy way of saying "patch." Here, your patch takes the shape of a skull, a star, a tomato, a poodle, or whatever. Take old boxer shorts, striped shirts, or forgotten plaid skirts and wear pieces of them in a new and exciting place.

MATERIALS

PAPER, FOR TEMPLATE

SCRAP FABRIC, FOR PATCHES

T-SHIRT

EMBROIDERY FLOSS IN A CONTRASTING COLOR

SEQUINS, BUTTONS, OR OTHER DECORATIVE ELEMENTS (optional)

TOOLS

PENCIL OR PEN

IRON (if fabric is wrinkled)

SCISSORS

STRAIGHT PINS

EMBROIDERY NEEDLE

Getting ready

Most fabric stores have a scrap bin, but it's cheaper and more fun to raid your own closet. Cottons and cotton blends (light denim, gingham, and the like) work best because the appliqué can weather the wash as well as the T-shirt. You can try other fabrics if they are not too thick nor stretchy nor knit—but you might end up hand-washing the tee. Fair enough?

How-to

1 **Make paper template.** On paper, draw the shape you want to appliqué. Keep it simple—a cloud, a teacup, a fish. Photocopy and cut out the scary skull using the template on page 56, if you like.

2 **Cut out shape from fabric.** Iron your fabric scrap if it's wrinkled. Lay the template on the fabric and trace around it. Cut out the shape, keeping the scissors just inside the line you made.

3 **Fray the edges.** Fray the edges of the fabric by poking a pin tip a few threads in from the edge and pulling the pin toward the edge until it

breaks through. Do this over and over, all around the edges until you are happy with the fringy border. Neaten up fringe with scissors, if you like.

4 Pin patch into place. Making sure that both patch and tee are lying flat, pin the patch into place. Don't stretch the tee under the patch. Take care to pin through only one layer of the tee. Carefully try on the T-shirt at this stage to make sure the appliqué hits you in the right spot.

5 Sew on patch. Thread your needle with embroidery floss. Sew a running stitch (see page 116) about ⅓ inch in from the edge of the patch.

6 Embellish further, if you want. Add sequins and buttons. Embroider flourishes. You can also layer several different fabrics to make an appliqué collage.

BABY TALK

Take a boring old onesie and add on fruit, a bunny, a duck, or a Trans Am. Or **appliqué a big design** to the back of a jeans jacket—or right onto your jeans.

KNOT • AGAIN

Modern-day macramé bracelet

Sailors and flower children do not have exclusive rights to macramé. Take this ancient (as in thousands of years old) craft into the new millennium with new materials. Washers and nuts from the hardware store make your jewelry modern and industrial—fit for a robot or a rock star.

HALF•TIME

You may think you're learning one macramé knot for this project, but you are actually learning two. If you repeat steps a and b from page 62 over and over (skipping c and d), you're making a half knot. If you make lots of half knots, they will twist to form a pretty spiral (check out the bracelet on the far left on page 61).

Getting ready

If you have never done macramé before, it's wise to cut two pieces of twine or take two shoelaces and try steps 2 through 4 with those. You'll get a little knot practice on a larger scale. This should save you time and errors later.

How-to

1 **Cut waxed linen cord.** Cut one piece of cord 20 inches long. Cut another one 72 inches long.

2 **Make a starting loop.** Pick one small nut to be your end-button and set it aside. Fold each cord in half to find the middle point. Holding the cords together, make a knot at the fold to form a starting loop (as shown at right). Before you tighten the knot, make sure the loop it forms can slip over your end-button, like a button and a button loop. Make sure it's not too snug or too loose.

3 **Prepare your work board.** Pin the starting loop to your corkboard near the top. Separate the two shorter cords (holding cords) from the two longer cords (working cords). Grasp the two holding cords and, keeping them taut, stick a pin in them about 6 inches below the starting loop or wind them figure-eight style around two pins as shown. The working cords are long, and it helps to get the excess out of your way. Take the end of one long cord and wind it around three fingers until there are about 15 inches left. Twist and pinch the loop of wound cord—the wax will hold it. Repeat with the other long cord.

starting loop

holding
cords

working cord

working cord

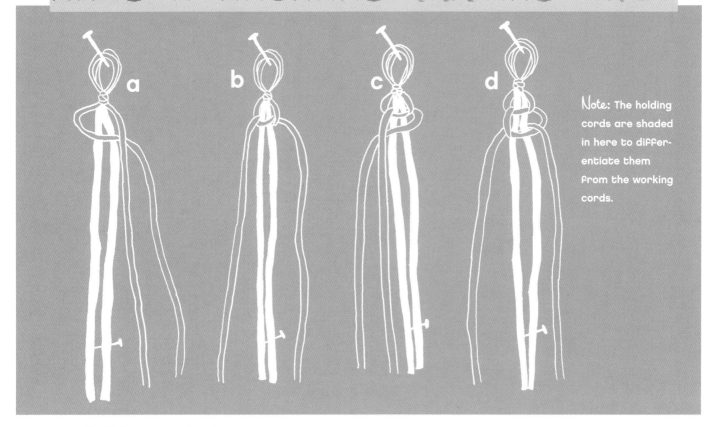

Note: The holding cords are shaded in here to differentiate them from the working cords.

Make square knots. In this form of macramé, the active working cords make knot after knot around the passive holding cords. Here's how:

a. Take the working cord from the left and lay it horizontally across the holding cords. Take the working cord from the right and lay it over the horizontal cord. The working cords now form the number 4.

b. Take the right-hand working cord and bring it under the holding cords and then up through the loop on the left. Pull the two working cords until the knot is tight and snug against the knot above.

c. Take the working cord that's now on the right, and lay it horizontally across the holding cords. Take the working cord on the left and lay it over the horizontal cord. The working cords now form a backward number 4.

d. Take the cord that's lying vertically and bring it under the holding cords and up through the loop on the right. Pull the two working cords until the knot is tight and snug against the knot above.

You have now made a complete macramé square knot. Repeat steps 4a through 4d until you want to add a hardware "bead."

NECK AND NECK

To create a **macramé choker,** cut a piece of waxed linen cord that is 45 inches long. Cut another one 4 yards long. Follow the directions for the bracelet, only keep knotting until you have 15 inches of macramé, centering your hardware decorations at the 7½-inch point.

(To do this you'll have to unwind all the excess working cord to get access to the ends.) Make sure you can't push the nut or washer over the overhand knot. Then take all four cords and make another overhand knot. Now the hardware is sandwiched securely between two big knots.

6 Continue knotting and decorating.

After you reach the center point, make square knots and add decorations to mirror the first half of the bracelet. As you approach the finish (somewhere around 6 to 8 inches), try on the bracelet to check for proper length.

7 Finish off.

When you reach the desired length, make another overhand knot and, using the method from step 5, add the final end-button you set aside in step 1. Make sure the last overhand knot is very tight. Cut the cord ends and dab white glue or Krazy Glue over the ends so they don't unravel. Push the end-button through the starting loop to fasten the bracelet.

5 Add a nut or washer for decoration.

As you work, periodically hold the bracelet up to your wrist to assess when and where you want to add hardware. The finished bracelet will be about 7 inches long, so place your middle decoration at about 3½ inches.

To add a small hardware nut or washer, make an overhand knot with all four cords (like the one that formed the starting loop) and tighten it snugly up against the last macramé knot. Slide the nut or washer or a few of them at once over all four cords like a regular bead.

projects for your home

YOUR • NEST

SHAGGY·DOG·RUG

A treat for your floor

Who doesn't have a pile of has-been T-shirts lying around?

T-shirts for teams and clubs and bands. Let them be born again!

The Shaggy Dog Rug doesn't need any training, but you can pet

it, preferably with your bare feet. *Strips of T-shirt*

become thick faux fur—fur that goes from the floor to the

wash and back under your toes.

Getting ready

Any T-shirt can become rug fur. A cotton tee, a cotton/polyester tee, a tee with a giant iron-on decal that says "Cats: The Montana Touring Company." It can have a huge mustard stain. Doesn't matter—you can cut around parts you don't want. But do wash all the shirts before you start.

The design of the Shaggy Dog Rug depends largely on the colors you use. An all-black or all-white rug looks sophisticated. A random mixture of bright colors looks like confetti. You can make fat stripes or swirls of color. Anything more detailed than that (an initial, a heart) won't work. The "fur" is too long and floppy to create distinctive boundaries.

Before you begin, you might want to rent all the movies of Woody Allen or get the book-on-tape version of *Moby-Dick*. This project takes a while. Don't plan to do it all in one night. Break it up into several sessions. The reward will be a rug you can use for years.

How-to

Cut and prepare burlap. Make a rectangle about 30 inches long by 24 inches wide—bath-mat size. Fold masking tape over the edges to prevent them from fraying (see taped edges of rug on page 71). Take the marker and draw a line about 2 inches in from the edge all the way around—this will be the outer edge of the rug. Follow the grain of the burlap threads as you go. That will help keep the edges straight.

2 **Make T-shirt strips.** Take a T-shirt and cut the collar, bottom hem, and arms off. Along the bottom, make short vertical scissor snips about 1 inch apart. Use the cuts to tear the T-shirt into long strips from bottom hem to collar. Sometimes the T-shirts don't tear perfectly and a strip is wider at one end. That's fine unless it gets wider than about 2 inches (too wide to weave into the burlap) or narrower than ½ inch (too weak to wear well). Some T-shirts are just hard to tear. You can cut those into strips with scissors. Throw out strips that are less than 6 inches long. Cut off the frazzled ends of strips. The sides of the strips will curl in on themselves— let them.

3 **Build the rug edges.** Take a T-shirt strip, thread one corner into the yarn needle, and pull the strip partway through. Start in the upper left corner of your marked rug boundary. Poke the needle into the burlap, then grasp it on the other side and pull. The loose weave of the burlap fabric should let the strip through with some wiggling. Leave a tail of 4 inches or so on the other side (the front of the burlap). Then about ½ inch over from the hole you just created, poke the needle-and-strip back through to the front of the rug. You should have a short tail and a long tail with the needle still on it. Cut the long tail so it's about the length of the short tail. Tie the two tails together in a square knot (right over left, left over right—see page 97). If you still have 6 or more inches of T-shirt strip on your needle, you don't need to rethread. Repeat this step, following the marker line, to make a border of knotted tails all around the edge of your rug. Space the knots out so they are almost touching each other but not crowding, bunching, or puckering the burlap.

SHAG ON Try making **a round rug.** You can fill in the circle with vertical rows, or you can spiral the rows in circles from the outside in. If you want a bigger area rug, **make several small ones and sew them together.** The "fur" will hide the seams. Sew several square rugs into a long row for a hallway runner.

While the front will start to look a bit wild and chaotic, you can always flip your rug over and look at the back to see where you are and how your rows are doing. The rows can be crooked as long as the spaces between them are about even. Also, you can have several rows in progress at the same time—helps distribute the color if you are making a confetti-style rug.

4 **Fill in the "fur."** Thread another T-shirt strip onto the yarn needle. Start in the upper left corner (or upper right if you're a lefty) about an inch in from the knot border. Plant your first strip with the down-in and up-out technique as above, creating two new tails. This time, don't tie the ends together. If you knotted all these tails, the rug would be too lumpy. Continue installing strips so they form a vertical row. Place them fairly close together—so they touch but not so close that the burlap buckles. This snugness will help lock the tails in place. Start the next vertical row of tails another inch or so toward the middle, parallel to the row you just made. Continue this process until no burlap shows on the front side.

5 **Finish and hide burlap edges.** Take the masking tape off and fold the raw burlap edges under once and then again. Pin in place. Then take a hand-sewing needle and strong thread and sew down the part that is pinned with a whipstitch or running stitch (see photo at right).

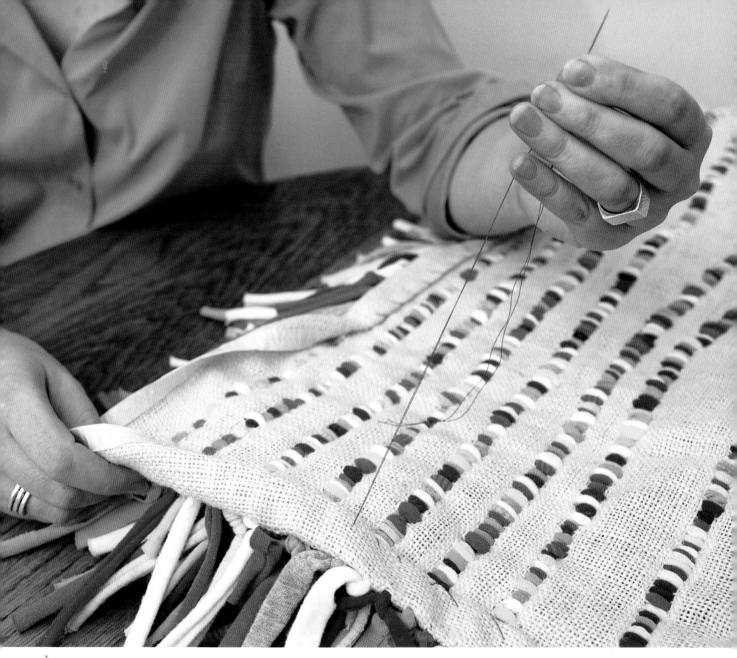

Steps 4 and 5: Fill in the "fur"
by threading T-shirt strips
into burlap in vertical rows
(see left). To finish, fold and
then sew down the burlap
edges (see above).

VEGGIE•PRINT•PILLOWCASES

Dream pretty

People have been **printing on fabric by hand** for centuries. Now you can too. Potatoes and carrots are cheap, easy to cut, and just porous enough to carry the dye to and fro. Toss out the veggies when you are done, and your **prints become truly limited editions.** Then you can look at your artwork each night **as you drift off to sleep.** Once you have this technique down, you can veggie-print all kinds of other things. Try T-shirts, curtains, tablecloths, or a whole set of sheets.

Steps 1-4: Cut stamps out
of potatoes and carrots,
dab paint onto the
stamps, then print.

MATERIALS

2 TO 8 WHITE OR OFF-
WHITE PREWASHED
PILLOWCASES (cotton or
cotton/poly blend)

1 TO 3 POTATOES

1 TO 3 CARROTS

WRITING PAPER OR
NEWSPAPER, FOR
TEMPLATES (optional)

FABRIC PAINT IN 2 OR 3
COLORS (Deka or Jacquard
brand, for example: available at
craft stores)

TOOLS

NEWSPAPER

PENCIL

SCISSORS

SHARP PARING KNIFE

HANDHELD ARTIST'S
CUTTING BLADE, SUCH AS
AN X-ACTO KNIFE (optional)

DISPOSABLE CONTAINERS
(like empty yogurt cups), 1 PER
COLOR OF PAINT

COTTON BALLS OR
ROUNDS

RAG

Getting ready

Starting with only two or three paint colors will save
you lots of color switching, which slows you down. Lay
out newspaper in the work area and wear old clothes.
Since you are setting up a little factory, it makes sense
to decorate several sets of pillowcases at once. You
can give the extras away as gifts.

How-to

1 **Design shapes for printing.** A sliced car-
rot makes a neat, natural circle—which is easy to
convert into a star or a sunburst with a few notches
around the edges. For bigger or more complicated
shapes (heart, rocket, seahorse, coffee cup), use the
potatoes. If you don't feel comfortable carving freehand, draw a template on a piece of paper first.
Remember that your template has to fit on the vegetable. Using scissors, cut out the paper template. If
you like this outer space motif, you can trace or photocopy and cut out the templates on page 76.

2 **Cut out shapes from veggies.** Using
the paring knife, cut the carrots crosswise. Using
the paring knife or an X-Acto blade, notch or cut the
edges into the desired shapes. Slice the potatoes

TIP

When you've been stamping with one color and you want to use that same stamp with a different color, wipe the old paint off with a damp rag, then stamp onto newspaper a couple of times until the color is gone (or very close to gone).

Smaller veggie stamps—especially ones cut from carrots—work wonderfully to customize cards and stationery. Just use inkpads meant for rubber stamping instead of using fabric paint.

4 Print. Pour a little of each paint color into its own disposable container. Take a cotton ball and dab it into a color. Then dab the paint onto the vegetable stamp. (You can use a paintbrush, but it leaves brushstrokes.) Press the stamp facedown onto a piece of newspaper to practice your stamping technique. Press the stamp a little so that the whole surface touches the newspaper, but don't wiggle it—that can lead to smearing. Lift the stamp up carefully. When ready, start stamping the pillowcases. Keep printing until you have decorated all of the fronts to your satisfaction. As cotton balls get oversoaked with paint, use new ones. If you want to do more printing later, wipe off the veggie stamps, wrap them in plastic, and store them in the refrigerator. They will last a few days.

5 Lock in color with heat. After the pillowcases have dried for a few hours or overnight, iron them according to the directions on the fabric paint jar. Usually you set the iron on high and iron over small areas of the pillowcase for 30 seconds at a time—always keep the iron moving. This step prevents the color from washing out.

crosswise for circles or the long way for more surface area. For bigger, more complicated stamps, lay the paper template on the potato surface. The moisture of the potato will hold the template in place. Trace the shape with the tip of a paring knife tip or X-Acto knife, cutting at least ½ inch deep. Then carve away the potato all around the shape, cutting about ½ inch deep (see carved potatoes on page 75). You basically end up with a big, perishable rubber stamp.

3 Line pillowcases. Put a few layers of newspaper inside each pillowcase so the fabric paint doesn't soak through. You can work on several pillowcases at a time if you have room to lay them out flat.

BUTTON · MOSAIC · FLOWERPOT

A container that blooms

A mosaic lets you create pictures with solid little nuggets of color. Traditionally those nuggets are glass or ceramic tiles, but you can use buttons. They are made in a huge variety of colors, textures, and finishes. And the repeated circles have a modern feel. This project takes time and patience, but the resulting artwork will last for years, indoors or out.

MATERIALS

GLAZED CERAMIC
FLOWERPOT

LOTS OF FLAT BUTTONS

TILE GLUE

TILE GROUT (without added sand)

TOOLS

NEWSPAPER

SANDPAPER (any grade)

PENCIL OR PEN

PLASTIC KNIVES

RAG

TOOTHPICKS

DISPOSABLE PLASTIC
CONTAINER (if you are mixing your own grout)

RUBBER GLOVES

OLD METAL NAIL FILE
OR LARGE HARDWARE
NAIL

OLD TOOTHBRUSH

Getting ready

First, a note on flowerpots. They are usually made out of terra-cotta (that red-brown clay), which is porous and helps plants absorb water. That's good news for the plants, but all that moisture would eventually break down the grout of your mosaic. So look in a hardware store or garden center for a flowerpot with a glazed ceramic finish. (Your plants will still be fine.) Plastic pots won't work either because they are too bendy—your mosaic would crack.

Buttons? You need a lot of them. Sometimes you can find buttons by the bagful at flea markets or sewing stores. Flat buttons work best, so take out the ones with a big nub (called a "shank") in the back. (You can save those for the Stitch-O-Licious Sachet project on page 112.) Separate your buttons into bowls—one for each color. This will be your artist's palette.

Lay out newspaper in your work area and make sure there is good ventilation. You don't want to breathe fumes from tile glue in a stuffy room.

How-to

1 **Prepare the flowerpot surface.** Rub the outside of the flowerpot with sandpaper. The scratches will help the glue adhere better.

2 **Plan your design.** Before you begin the mosaic, plan your pattern. (Unless you feel confident enough to make a pattern on the fly—that's fine too.) On a piece of newspaper, draw a square about the

Steps 3-6: After gluing buttons over the entire flowerpot, let dry. Then smear with grout and wipe away excess.

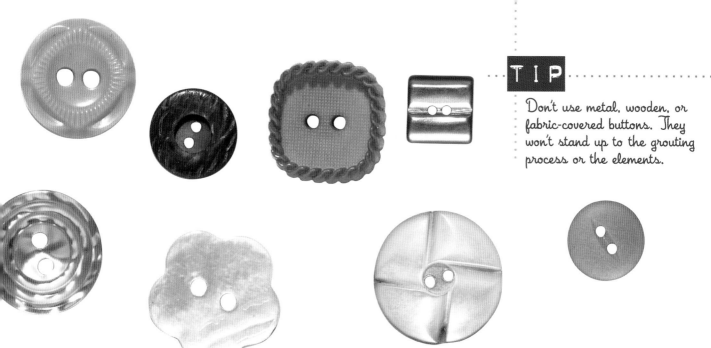

TIP

Don't use metal, wooden, or fabric-covered buttons. They won't stand up to the grouting process or the elements.

height and width of your flowerpot and arrange the buttons to form your pattern or design, filling the square. This gives you a sense of how the circles will lie next to each other. Fill in gaps with more buttons. Use buttons to draw a picture, make a monogram, create bands of color, or make a random button mishmash. All-one-color-button pots look great too.

3 **Spread the tile glue.** Use the plastic knife to spread tile glue over a small area of the pot—about 3 inches square—as if you were spreading jam on bread. You don't want the layer of glue to be thicker than the buttons or they will sink in too far. But make it thick enough for the buttons to stick. Experiment to find a happy medium. If the glue starts to dry before you cover an area, just apply more.

4 **Cover the flowerpot with buttons.** Arrange the buttons in the glue as they were in your practice square on the table. You have time to move buttons after you have placed them, so you can prod and adjust until you are happy. Try not to get glue on the button fronts (if you do, wipe it off with a damp rag). The glue sometimes oozes through the buttonholes. When it does, either wipe it away with a damp rag or poke the end of a toothpick into the hole and lift out the excess glue (sounds weird, but it's actually neater and easier than wiping). Once you feel the glue starting to set, leave the buttons alone. After you have covered one gluey area, spread glue and place buttons on an adjacent patch. Repeat until the pot is covered. Don't bring the mosaic to the very edges of your pot. Leave at least ⅓ inch of space near the top and bottom for the grout.

SUPER•SCRAPER

To make the scraping go faster, leave the work area. Put your pot on a plastic plate or tray (to catch the grout dust) and work in front of the TV or on the couch while you chat on the phone.

5 **Let dry.** Place the flowerpot upside down and leave it overnight.

6 **Apply grout.** Some grout comes as premixed putty, some as a powder (which is cheaper because you mix it yourself). If you are mixing your own grout, make it in a plastic disposable container, and stir until it's about as thick as pudding. You can always add more water or powder to adjust. Wearing gloves to protect your hands, and with the pot still upside down on the table, take a plastic knife or your gloved finger and scoop up some grout. Wipe it over a small section of buttons—as much as that glob of grout will cover. Then with knife tip or fingertip, work the grout into all the cracks and crevices between the buttons and into the buttons' holes. Then take a damp rag and wipe off the excess grout. Wipe off as much as you can—the more excess grout you can get off now, the less you have to scrape off later. Repeat on the next area, then the next, until the entire mosaic is grouted.

7 **Let dry and scrape.** Dry the pot upside down overnight as before. When it's dry, it will probably look like something that just emerged from an archaeological dig—with the buttons still a little buried in grout. Use the point of an old metal nail file or hardware nail, or other small sharp tool (even your thumbnail) to scrape away a small area of excess grout. Then brush with an old toothbrush. Move to another small area of the mosaic and repeat. This step can take a long time, but it goes faster if you pretend you are an archaeologist uncovering a treasure—except it's a treasure you made yourself.

8 **Touch up.** If there are cracks or gaps or missed spots, fill them in with a little wet grout, wipe off the excess, and let dry overnight before scraping and brushing clean.

OTHER (EVEN EASIER) MOSAICS

You can use the same glue-and-grout technique with **colored glass pebbles** sold for gardens and fish tanks. Or try **polished river stones** in pretty, earthy tones. These materials are smooth and solid. Not a gardener? Make your mosaic on an old wooden picture frame.

COWBOY•CURTAINS

The all-American bandana

can do more than decorate your head during an Ultimate Frisbee game. It's a great building block for textile projects—and you don't have to hem a thing. Let the sun shine through these curtains fit for a cowboy.

MATERIALS

15 TO 20 BANDANAS PER CURTAIN (cotton or cotton/poly, as long as all are the same)

SEWING THREAD (IN A MATCHING OR NEUTRAL COLOR)

TENSION ROD OR OTHER ROD-AND-BRACKET SETUP (available at hardware stores)

TOOLS

YARDSTICK OR TAPE MEASURE

POST-IT NOTES (optional)

STRAIGHT PINS

HAND-SEWING NEEDLE OR SEWING MACHINE

IRON

Getting ready

Most bandanas are about 16 inches or 21 inches square. The bigger ones give you more curtain with less sewing. On the other hand, the smaller bandanas let you make fancier patchwork patterns. Works either way.

Traditional bandanas come in fire-truck red and navy blue. These colors look great together, especially in a masculine room. But if you look around (army-navy stores are a good source), you can find bandanas in all kinds of pastel colors that make light and airy curtains.

Traditional seamstress types would tell you to wash and iron all the bandanas ahead of time, but this is a royal pain. It's easier to wash and iron the whole thing after it's done, so keep in mind that if your bandanas are all-cotton, they will shrink about 5 to 10 percent after the first washing—less if you keep them out of the dryer. Cotton/polyester bandanas shouldn't shrink at all (or very little).

How-to

1 **Measure the window and plan curtain size.** The rule of thumb for curtain width is to take the width of the window and at least double it. For example, our window on page 86 is 51 inches wide and the bandanas are about 22 inches across. So

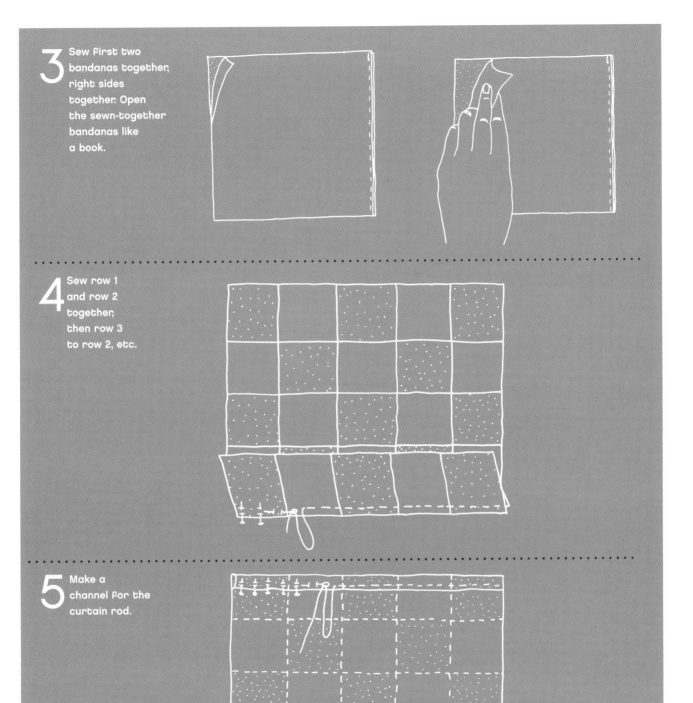

3 Sew first two bandanas together, right sides together. Open the sewn-together bandanas like a book.

4 Sew row 1 and row 2 together, then row 3 to row 2, etc.

5 Make a channel for the curtain rod.

EXPAND YOUR BANDANA EMPIRE

You can follow the exact same instructions (minus steps 5 and 6) to make **a bedspread**. Or sew the bedspread to a twin- or full-sized sheet on three sides, then sew three or four snaps along the open, short side, and you have a duvet cover. Stitch together two bandanas for a complementary throw pillow. If you want to Westernize your kitchen, sew a grid of three bandanas by three bandanas for **a cute tablecloth**. Then use individual bandanas as napkins.

five bandanas add up to 110 inches across—double the window width plus a little extra. The height of the window is 66 inches, so the curtain needs to be four bandanas— or 88 inches—long. This gives a little extra fabric for seam allowances and the curtain rod channel at the top. It's fine for a curtain to hang down the wall a bit. You can even make your curtains long enough to touch the floor.

2 **Lay out your pattern.** Once you know how many bandanas you need, lay them out like a giant grid in the middle of the floor. Try different patterns. A basic two-color checkerboard pattern works really well. Diagonal stripes (shown on page 86) are easy. And a random mosaic of colors looks like modern art. Think of it as a patchwork quilt with big patches. Don't forget that the curtain will be bunched up when it's hanging in the window, so keep the design simple.

3 **Sew bandanas into rows.** Once you have the grid set up, think of it as several horizontal rows of squares. Look at the top row and, starting with the top left and going right, number the squares in your head (or use Post-it Notes) from 1 to 5 (or however many you have). Start with the bandanas numbered 1 and 2. Place them right sides together, line them up along the right edge, and pin together. Sew along that edge just inside the bandanas' tiny hems (see diagram on page 89). This way you only go through two layers of fabric. Use a running stitch (see page 116) if you are

HANKY • PLEASE

For curtains in a baby's room (or for a delicate touch in a grown-up's room), sew together vintage embroidered handkerchiefs. You can find them in thrift stores or maybe at your grandmother's house. Cut them all to the same size, preserving the embroidered corner, and patch together. Or leave them whole and lay them on the ground, moving them around until they form a big rectangle (or close to it). Stitch the hankies together, then make a curtain rod channel as in step 5, or buy café curtain rings that clip into place.

working by hand or a straight stitch if you are sewing by machine. Open the squares like a book (as shown on page 89) and place them back into the grid right side up, with the seam allowance toward the floor. Then take bandana number 3 and place it right sides together with bandana number 2. Pin together along the right edges so the new seam is parallel to the first seam. Sew together. Continue in the same way, sewing square number 4 to square number 3 and so on, until you have

reached the end of the row. It's like you are adding links to a chain of squares. When the row is complete, iron it flat. Press the seam allowances toward the darker color. Place the row back in the grid and repeat the process for each row of squares in the grid.

4 **Sew the rows together.** Keeping the rows in grid formation, number them in your head (or use Post-it Notes) from top to bottom. Take row number 1 and flip it facedown onto row number 2. Pin the edges together and then sew them, running the seam just inside the bandanas' tiny hems. Open the fabric back up, return it to the grid right side up with the seam toward the floor. Make sure that your overall pattern still looks right. Flip row 3 up so that it lies face-down on top of row number 2. Pin and stitch along the bottom edge as before. Continue until you have sewed the complete curtain face together. Iron it flat, pressing the seam allowances to one side.

5 **Make a channel for the curtain rod.** Fold the top edge of the curtain back toward the wrong side about 2 inches (more if you are using a big curtain rod) and pin it into place. Sew straight across near the edge.

6 **Hang the curtain.** You can use any kind of rod, but a tension rod is easiest. Thread the rod through the channel at the curtain top. Place the rod inside the window well.

PLACES•EVERYONE!

Chopstick place mats

Chopsticks have graced tables for thousands of years. But in a new twist, serve them up as place mats. Just tie them together with waxed linen cord and beads—like a pretty raft for your plate to float upon.

DOES • SIZE • MATTER?

A 20-chopstick-wide place mat is smaller than the mats you see in stores. But it's big enough to hold a dinner plate off the table—which is the function of a place mat—and it's got pleasing proportions. If you want to go wider, then add five or more chopsticks.

Getting ready

In planning your place mats, you can go natural with plain wooden chopsticks, off-white linen cord, and wooden or clear-glass beads. Or make your place mats colorful and modern. Use black or red lacquered chop-sticks, waxed linen in bright jewel tones, and any col-orful beads that excite you. This project takes a bit of time, but you can do it in front of the TV—and the result is a place mat set that no one else in the world will have.

How-to

1 **Cut waxed linen cord.** Cut eight cords each 2 yards long (two cords per place mat).

2 **Set up knotting.** Take one cord and fold it in half to find the middle. Place the middle of the cord 2 inches from the end of a chopstick and wrap it around twice. Pull tight (you'll need to make sure to pull tight at every step) and tie a square knot (see right). With another cord, do the same thing at the other end of the chopstick, 2 inches in.

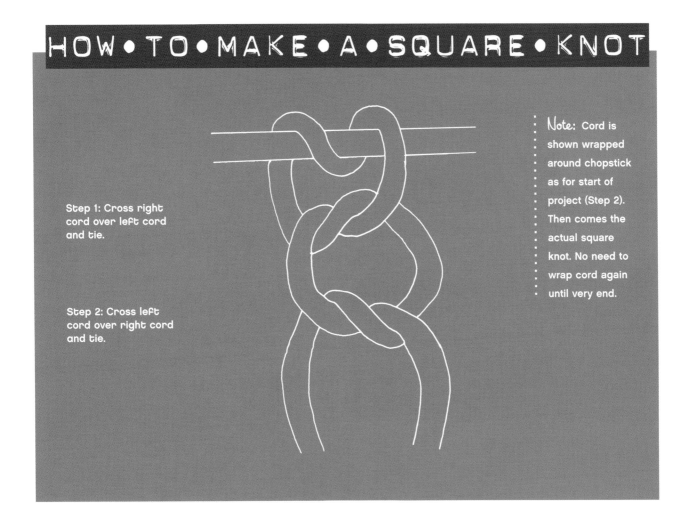

Step 1: Cross right cord over left cord and tie.

Step 2: Cross left cord over right cord and tie.

Note: Cord is shown wrapped around chopstick as for start of project (Step 2). Then comes the actual square knot. No need to wrap cord again until very end.

3 **Thread beads.** At one end of the chopstick, take the two cord-ends that just formed a square knot, and thread a bead onto both as if they were one cord. (It helps to line up the cord-ends and smush them together so the wax makes them into one pointy end for bead-threading.) Push the bead right up to the square knot. You can put two beads on if you want your chopsticks spaced farther apart. Feel free to experiment. Make a square knot on the other side of bead to hold it in place. Repeat process at the other end of the chopstick.

Steps 3-5: Alternate chopsticks and beads, held
together with square
knots, to build place mat.

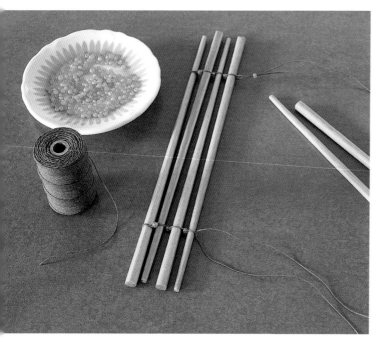

Put a new chopstick in place. Chopsticks have one fat end that tapers down to a narrower end. If the first chopstick in your place mat has the fat end on the left, then place the second chopstick with the fat end on the right. Alternate chopstick directions throughout the project so your place mat will be rectangular and your plate will sit flat.

Tie in a new chopstick. Take the two waxed linen cords from one end and bring one of them over and the other under the new chopstick. Tie the first half of the square knot. Make sure the ends of the first and second chopstick line up, then finish the square knot, pulling tightly. Repeat at the other end.

Repeat steps 3 though 5. Stop when you place your twentieth chopstick.

Finish. On your last chopstick, wrap one of the linen cords around the stick twice. Then tie it to the other cord right snug up to the last bead as shown in the photo at right. Pull the knot very tight, cut off the ends of the cord, and secure the tips with a dab of white glue.

TIP

Most chopsticks are carved or molded with some squareness—like a railroad tie instead of a pole. When you're placing a chopstick, try to make sure the flat side, not a corner, will rest on the table. It doesn't really matter, but looks a little nicer and lies flatter on the table this way.

Step 7: When you reach the last chopstick, wrap one of the cords around twice, then tie it to the other cord close to the last bead.

BURNING • FOR • YOU

Woodburned cutting board

Bring an old summer-camp craft into the kitchen by woodburning

a cutting board. It's almost as easy as

drawing with a pencil (okay, a really, really HOT pencil).

Go antique-y or super-mod. Takes less than an hour.

MATERIALS

SCRAP WOOD (optional)

WOODEN CUTTING BOARD

STENCIL (optional)

CARDBOARD OR CARD
STOCK (optional)

TOOLS

PENCIL

WOODBURNING TOOL
(available at craft supply stores,
comes as a kit with several
nibs)

ERASER

PLIERS (optional)

BURN • ON

If you want to get your money's worth from your woodburning tool, try decorating the outside of a wooden salad bowl. Make matching tongs. Craft stores also sell wooden boxes and plaques you can customize with your sizzling new skills.

Getting ready

The most important part of getting ready is practicing with the tool. Heat up the woodburner and try some lines and designs on a piece of scrap wood—preferably made of hardwood similar to your cutting board. Notice the difference between making straight and curved lines (curved lines are harder). The standard tip on a woodburning tool is shaped like a lopsided wedge. You can just stick with the main tip or try others in the kit, if you like. Use the pointy end for fine lines. Use the wide edge for wide lines and shading. A rounded tip makes curved lines easier. When changing points, let the tool cool off completely and unscrew the tip with pliers, not your fingers. If you don't have pliers available, wait extra long before changing tips and use a hot pad.

How-to

1 **Draw your design in pencil.** If you are feeling brave, freehand it. Use the lightest pencil marks that you can still see. If you make a mistake, you can erase the line and try again. If you want more help, use a stencil from a stationery store, or cut a template from cardboard or card stock and trace around it. Keep your design simple.

2 **Woodburn over the pencil design.** Be sure you've practiced with the tool first. You can always add lines, but you cannot subtract them. Moving the tool quickly will create a lighter line. Moving slowly will make a darker line. If you make a mistake, just incorporate it into the design. It might become your favorite part.

3 **Erase any traces of pencil.**

WOODBURNING•SAMPLER

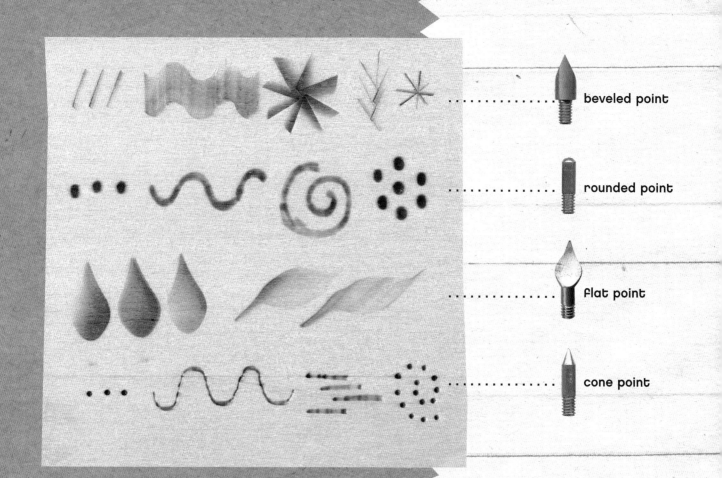

beveled point

rounded point

flat point

cone point

PROJECTS•TO•GIVE••PROJECTS•TO•GIVE••PROJECTS•TO•GIVE••PROJECTS•TO•GIVE••PROJECTS•TO•
••PROJECTS•TO•GIVE••PROJECTS•TO•GIVE••PROJECTS•TO•GIVE••PROJECTS•TO•GIVE••PROJECTS•T
VE•PROJECTS•TO•GIVE••PROJECTS•TO•GIVE••PROJECTS•TO•GIVE•PROJECTS•TO•GIVE••PROJECTS•
IVE••PROJECTS•TO•GIVE•PROJECTS•TO•GIVE••PROJECTS•TO•GIVE••PROJECTS•TO•GIVE•PROJECTS
GIVE••PROJECTS•TO•GIVE••PROJECTS•TO•GIVE•PROJECTS•TO•GIVE••PROJECTS•TO•GIVE••PROJECT
O•GIVE•PROJECTS•TO•GIVE••PROJECTS•TO•GIVE••PROJECTS•TO•GIVE•PROJECTS•TO•GIVE••PROJ-
ECTS•TO•GIVE••PROJECTS•TO•GIVE•PROJECTS•TO•GIVE••PROJECTS•TO•GIVE••PROJECTS•TO•GIVE
JECTS•TO•GIVE••PROJECTS•TO•GIVE••PROJECTS•TO•GIVE•PROJECTS•TO•GIVE••PROJECTS•TO•GIV
ROJECTS•TO•GIVE•PROJECTS•TO•GIVE••PROJECTS•TO•GIVE••PROJECTS•TO•GIVE•PROJECTS•TO•GI
PROJECTS•TO•GIVE••PROJECTS•TO•GIVE•PROJECTS•TO•GIVE••PROJECTS•TO•GIVE••PROJECTS•TO•
••PROJECTS•TO•GIVE••PROJECTS•TO•GIVE••PROJECTS•TO•GIVE•PROJECTS•TO•GIVE••PROJECTS•TO
E••PROJECTS•TO•GIVE•PROJECTS•TO•GIVE••PROJECTS•TO•GIVE••PROJECTS•TO•GIVE•PROJECTS•T
VE••PROJECTS•TO•GIVE••PROJECTS•TO•GIVE•PROJECTS•TO•GIVE••PROJECTS•TO•GIVE••PROJECTS
GIVE•PROJECTS•TO•GIVE••PROJECTS•TO•GIVE••PROJECTS•TO•GIVE•PROJECTS•TO•GIVE••PROJECT
•GIVE••PROJECTS•TO•GIVE•PROJECTS•TO•GIVE••PROJECTS•TO•GIVE••PROJECTS•TO•GIVE•PROJEC
O•GIVE••PROJECTS•TO•GIVE••PROJECTS•TO•GIVE•PROJECTS•TO•GIVE••PROJECTS•TO•GIVE••PROJ
ECTS•TO•GIVE•PROJECTS•TO•GIVE••PROJECTS•TO•GIVE••PROJECTS•TO•GIVE•PROJECTS•TO•GIVE•
JECTS•TO•GIVE••PROJECTS•TO•GIVE•PROJECTS•TO•GIVE••PROJECTS•TO•GIVE••PROJECTS•TO•GIV
OJECTS•TO•GIVE••PROJECTS•TO•GIVE••PROJECTS•TO•GIVE•PROJECTS•TO•GIVE••PROJECTS•TO•GI
PROJECTS•TO•GIVE•PROJECTS•TO•GIVE••PROJECTS•TO•GIVE••PROJECTS•TO•GIVE•PROJECTS•TO•G
•PROJECTS•TO•GIVE••PROJECTS•TO•GIVE•PROJECTS•TO•GIVE••PROJECTS•TO•GIVE••PROJECTS•TO
E•PROJECTS•TO•GIVE••PROJECTS•TO•GIVE••PROJECTS•TO•GIVE•PROJECTS•TO•GIVE••PROJECTS•T
VE••PROJECTS•TO•GIVE•PROJECTS•TO•GIVE••PROJECTS•TO•GIVE••PROJECTS•TO•GIVE•PROJECTS•
IVE••PROJECTS•TO•GIVE••PROJECTS•TO•GIVE•PROJECTS•TO•GIVE••PROJECTS•TO•GIVE••PROJECT
•GIVE•PROJECTS•TO•GIVE••PROJECTS•TO•GIVE••PROJECTS•TO•GIVE•PROJECTS•TO•GIVE••PROJEC
O•GIVE••PROJECTS•TO•GIVE•PROJECTS•TO•GIVE••PROJECTS•TO•GIVE••PROJECTS•TO•GIVE•PROJ-
ECTS•TO•GIVE••PROJECTS•TO•GIVE••PROJECTS•TO•GIVE•PROJECTS•TO•GIVE••PROJECTS•TO•GIVE
OJECTS•TO•GIVE•PROJECTS•TO•GIVE••PROJECTS•TO•GIVE••PROJECTS•TO•GIVE•PROJECTS•TO•GIV
ROJECTS•TO•GIVE••PROJECTS•TO•GIVE•PROJECTS•TO•GIVE••PROJECTS•TO•GIVE••PROJECTS•TO•G
PROJECTS•TO•GIVE••PROJECTS•TO•GIVE••PROJECTS•TO•GIVE•PROJECTS•TO•GIVE••PROJECTS•TO•
••PROJECTS•TO•GIVE•PROJECTS•TO•GIVE••PROJECTS•TO•GIVE••PROJECTS•TO•GIVE•PROJECTS•TO
E••PROJECTS•TO•GIVE••PROJECTS•TO•GIVE•PROJECTS•TO•GIVE••PROJECTS•TO•GIVE••PROJECTS•
IVE•PROJECTS•TO•GIVE••PROJECTS•TO•GIVE••PROJECTS•TO•GIVE•PROJECTS•TO•GIVE••PROJECTS
GIVE••PROJECTS•TO•GIVE•PROJECTS•TO•GIVE••PROJECTS•TO•GIVE••PROJECTS•TO•GIVE•PROJECT
•GIVE••PROJECTS•TO•GIVE••PROJECTS•TO•GIVE•PROJECTS•TO•GIVE••PROJECTS•TO•GIVE••PROJ-
ECTS•TO•GIVE••PROJECTS•TO•GIVE•PROJECTS•TO•GIVE••PROJECTS•TO•GIVE••PROJECTS•TO•GIVE•
JECTS•TO•GIVE••PROJECTS•TO•GIVE•PROJECTS•TO•GIVE••PROJECTS•TO•GIVE••PROJECTS•TO•GIV

YOUR•FRIENDS
AND•FAMILY

projects to give

PIN-TASTIC•CARDS

Fast. Easy. Impressive. Totally fun.

Take out your aggression on an innocent piece of card stock.

In about five minutes you can **customize birthday**

cards, notes, love letters. And you probably have

all the supplies you'll need already.

MATERIALS

LIGHTWEIGHT PAPER OR
VELLUM, FOR TEMPLATE

HEAVY PAPER (card stock,
construction paper, or blank
index cards)

ENVELOPE (optional)

TOOLS

PENCIL

PINKING SHEARS OR
DECORATIVE PAPER
EDGERS (optional)

OLD MOUSE PAD, CORK
BOARD, OR LARGE PIECE
STYROFOAM, TO USE AS
A WORK SURFACE

PUSHPIN

Getting ready

Paper piercing is a traditional technique used to decorate lampshades and to make paper lacy. But for all the fancy lineage, we're really just talking about stabbing paper with a pin. Purists use a special piercing tool that looks more like a pencil and offers a little more control. But a pushpin from your bulletin board works just fine.

In planning your design, start with simple letters (see the alphabet on page 110), lines, or drawings. If you want a monogram or thank-you message, type it on your computer in a font that you like and print it out big. Look in magazines, newspapers, even commercial cards for words and images to turn into dotted lines. Or make up your own design—experiment in pencil until you come up with something that moves you.

How-to

1 **Make a template.** Draw, trace, or print out your design onto lightweight paper or vellum. Enlarge the text or images on a photocopier, if necessary.

2 **Prepare card.** Fold and cut the heavy paper or card stock to a size you like or to the proper size for the envelope. Cut a decorative edge, if desired.

A B C D E F G H I

J K L M N O P Q R

S T U V W X Y Z

3 **Set up your piercing station.** Place the card to be pierced on top of firm yet spongy padding (an old mouse pad or some Styrofoam or cork board). Place the template on top of the card, centering it or eyeballing the best position. Hold the template in place with your free hand. Or, for hands-free piercing, you can hold your template in place with pushpins in the four corners of the card, then incorporate the holes into your design.

4 **Pierce design.** Using a pushpin, pierce along the lines of your template, poking straight down—not at an angle. A good rule of thumb: The space between holes should be at least as wide as the holes themselves. If the holes are too close together, the card can tear. If the holes are too far apart, you lose the sense of a line. Experiment. If you are feeling confident, embellish with freehand dots and swirls.

REVERSE • DECISION

For a more 3-D sculptural effect, try piercing from back to front. The holes will have nice raised edges. If you are piercing from the back and making words or letters, your template needs to have a reverse image. Trace your design onto sheer paper and flip it over.

HOLE-Y HOLIDAYS

Pierce **custom gift tags** with names and monograms. Make **holiday cards** with pushpin snow. Like Cupid, pierce hearts for Valentine's Day.

STITCH-O-LICIOUS•SACHET

An old shirt plus some buttons

and embroidery thread and you can be a Jane Austen character

for a day—stitching away while discussing your future spouse or

that motorcycle trip you've been thinking about. The basic

embroidery techniques here can soothe the savage mind and

decorate just about anything made of fabric.

Steps 3-6: After embellishing with buttons and embroidery, sew the two sides of the sachet together, leaving an opening for adding filling.

MATERIALS

HEAVY PAPER (such as grocery bag paper), FOR TEMPLATE

OLD COTTON SHIRT IN OXFORD CLOTH, LIGHT DENIM, OR CORDUROY

ASSORTED BUTTONS

COTTON EMBROIDERY FLOSS IN ASSORTED COLORS

THREAD IN A MATCHING OR CONTRASTING COLOR (optional)

SACHET FILLER SUCH AS LAVENDER, CHAMOMILE TEA, OR MINT TEA (available at craft stores or gourmet tea shops)

SMALL BEADS (optional)

TOOLS

PEN OR PENCIL

SCISSORS

IRON (if needed)

HAND-SEWING NEEDLE

CREWEL NEEDLE (or any needle big enough for embroidery floss)

STRAIGHT PINS

BIG FUNNEL (or extra paper to form a cone)

Getting ready

If you have never embroidered before, see the how-to instructions on pages 116-117, fear not. It's a lot like drawing, except you make lines with colorful thread instead of a pencil. There are some fancy stitches you can learn to create complex designs and textures, but even with the most basic of stitches, the results can be pretty great. The beauty of this sachet project is that the buttons do half the decorating. Almost any stitching around the buttons will turn them into flowers. Keep it simple, or combine stitches if you are feeling adventurous.

As for sachet fabric, men's work shirts are ideal, but any light- to medium-weight cotton is fine. Solid colors show off the embroidery best. The stripes (called "wales") of corduroy add nice texture. Don't pick fabric that's too thick, because the nice fragrance of the sachet filling can't come through as easily.

How-to

1   **Make template.** Fold a piece of heavy paper in half and draw half a heart at the folded edge. Cut both layers of paper along the line and unfold.

2 Cut heart shapes from fabric. Make sure the shirt you are cutting is wrinkle-free. Iron it, if necessary. Place the template on the fabric. Notice that the threads of the fabric run vertically and horizontally. Line up the center crease of the paper heart with one of the fabric threads, trace the heart shape with a pen, and cut it out. Don't worry if the marks show—they will be hidden in the end. Repeat this step to make a second fabric heart.

3 Sew buttons onto one heart. Use a crewel needle or hand-sewing needle and either embroidery floss or regular thread. Sew all the buttons on at once, or sew one whole button-and-flower combo (see step 4) at a time—everyday shirt buttons or interesting vintage ones work equally well. Where you place the second button might depend on how the first button-and-flower turns out.

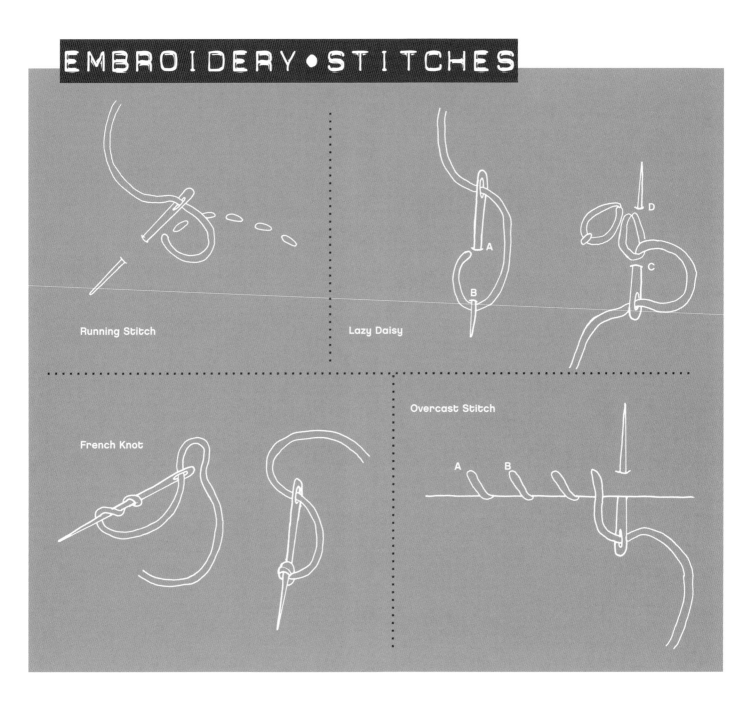

EMBROIDERY·STITCHES

Running Stitch

Lazy Daisy

French Knot

Overcast Stitch

STITCH-O-LICIOUS SACHET

RUNNING STITCH: Start at the back of the fabric, and bring the needle up and down to make a dotted line like the middle of the highway. You can make the stitches one at a time, or scoop up several on the needle in one go.

LAZY DAISY: This stitch is very easy. Pick a spot for the base of the flower petal, and bring the needle up—going from the back of the fabric to the front. Pull the thread through. Poke the needle back in very close to where the thread came up (A), but don't pull through yet. Bring the tip of the needle up where you want the pointy end of the petal to be (B; about ½ inch away, radiating out from the flower center). Now pull the thread through, catching the loop you just formed. Pull until the loop forms a small flower petal. (Don't pull the loop too tight or the fabric will pucker.) Poke the needle back down into the fabric to form a tiny stitch that holds the petal in place (C). Tie a knot or bring needle up where you want to start the next lazy daisy petal (D).

FRENCH KNOT: This stitch is harder, but makes pretty dots. Practice a few times on scrap fabric first. Bring the needle up from the back of the fabric and pull through. Holding the thread taut with your left hand (or everything in reverse for lefties), wrap the thread around the needle 2 or 3 times as shown. Then place the tip of needle back into the fabric very close to the spot you came up and carefully pull through. TIP: French knots are easier when the working embroidery floss is short—like 5 to 8 inches long.

OVERCAST STITCH: Also called a whip stitch, this must be worked near the edge of the fabric. Come up from the back of the fabric about ¼ inch in from the edge and pull the thread through. Move about a ½ inch over and bring the needle through again from back-to-front. The thread wraps around the edge on a diagonal. You can space the stitches closer to or farther from the edge or from each other—but keep them consistent.

TIP

Don't pull the stitches so tight that the fabric puckers. Traditional embroiderers put fabric in an embroidery hoop to hold it taut and pucker-free. You can skip the hoop if you stay aware of your stitch tension and pull the fabric taut with your fingers every now and then.

Step 6: Use a funnel or
paper cone to fill sachet,
then sew border and close
gap with overcast stitching.

Embroider flower petals. Thread your crewel needle with embroidery floss and embroider petals around the buttons. For the simplest (or at least easiest) flower, just spiral a running stitch around the button. The result looks like a rose or carnation. You can make two or three flowers like this in different colors and call it a day. To make oblong petals, use the lazy daisy stitch. French knots are a little trickier but look very delicate. Use single short stitches as fringy petals or use French knots to fill in lazy daisy petals. Combine stitches any way you like. Invent new stitches and petals.

Sew fabric hearts together. You now have two fabric hearts—one embroidered, one plain. Pin them right sides together. Using regular thread or spare embroidery floss (two strands thick) and the hand-sewing needle, make a running stitch around the edge of the hearts about ¼ inch from the edge, leaving an opening 1 to 2 inches wide so you can pour in the filling. You are basically making a little pillow.

Add filling. Turn your creation right side out. Use the funnel to help you pour the fragrant herbs or tea inside. Fill the heart two-thirds to three-quarters full.

Finish edges. Fold the raw edges of the opening inward about ¼ inch and, starting at one end of the opening, sew it closed using the overcast stitch. (Thread a bead onto every other stitch if you like.) Tie a knot in the back.

TABLE • TALK

Plant your embroidered flowers on a set of napkins. Buy any solid-colored cotton napkin set. Sew a button and petals on one corner of each. Let them match or make a garden variety.

NEWSPAPER•FLOWERS

The ultimate indoor garden

These flowers take about ten minutes to make and stay fresh for months—no watering required. Make whole bouquets—you'll be recycling newspapers in a way your city council never thought possible. Here man (or woman) imitates nature, only the man- or woman-made flower features a picture of the vice president or a mattress ad. Ha!

MATERIALS

NEWSPAPER

18-GAUGE WIRE (available at hardware stores)

CLEAR TAPE

FLORAL TAPE (available at florist or craft stores)

TOOLS

RULER

SCISSORS

PLIERS

WIRE CUTTERS

Steps 2 and 3: Four strategic folds and a few snips with a scissor yield the petals you need to create newspaper flowers.
Once you've got the process down, try cutting other petal shapes—spiky petals, long skinny daisy petals—and see what new flower species emerge.

Getting ready

Obviously, real flowers are not black and white, so using plain old newspaper has an interesting industrial effect. For more color, try one of the pink-tinted papers like the *Financial Times* or the *New York Observer*. Sunday comics offer interesting pastels. Magazines made of thin newspaper-grade paper—like *Parade* or the Sunday *New York Times Magazine*—work very well. Their pages have a sheen and lots of color photos. Regular newsstand magazines aren't suitable—the paper is too stiff, and the pages are too small.

How-to

Cut six newspaper squares. Cut six 9-inch squares. They can be a little bigger or smaller, if you like. They can be a little sloppy and imperfect since you will be cutting them into petals.

Fold squares. Take one square and fold it in half to form a triangle. Then fold that in half and in half again as shown at right. Take the small triangle, keeping the completely folded edge on the left, and fold it once more as shown to form an irregular triangle shape. Repeat with the other five newspaper squares.

Cut petals. Divide your folded triangles into two batches—three of them will form outer petals and three will be inner petals. For the outer petals, keep the folded edge to the right and cut an arc as shown—sort of an upside-down J. For the inner petals, either cut a shallow arc and then three 2-inch-long vertical snips as shown (a) or cut a double arc as shown (b).

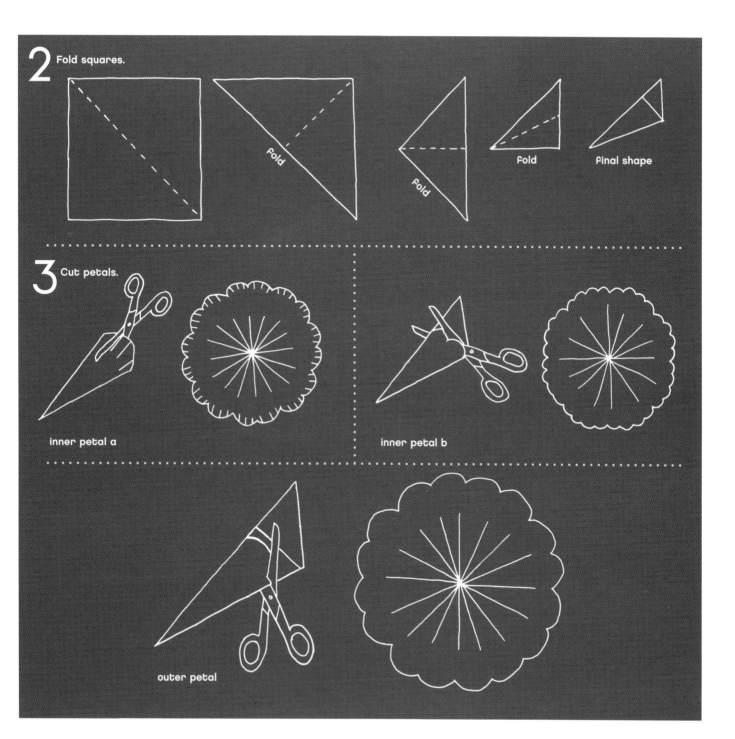

2 Fold squares.

Fold

Fold

Fold

Final shape

3 Cut petals.

inner petal a

inner petal b

outer petal

Step 6: Thread the petals onto the wire one by one. Below are version b inner petals (see page 123).

4 Unfold and stack layers of petals.
Unfold all six petal layers, but don't flatten them completely—the ridges from the folds will help the petals take shape. Stack the three outer petal layers on top of each other like plates, then stack the three inner petal layers on top of those.

5 Create stem. Cut about an 8-inch length of wire. Using pliers, bend a little loop at the top of the wire. This will be a brake to hold the petals in place on the stem.

6 Thread petals onto stem. Take the top petal layer (which is an inner petal) from the stack and pierce it in the center with the unbent end of the wire. Slide it to the bent end. Take the next petal layer and do the same. It's sort of like making a paper shish kebab. Repeat until the whole stack of paper is on the wire stem.

IN LIVING COLOR

While magazine pages are sophisti-cated, **Sunday comics** bloom in bright colors.

Step 9: Wind floral tape around the base of the flower, then down the wire stem.

7 **Close the flower.** This is the slightly tricky part, so take a little time with it. Gently smush the petals closed as if you were closing an umbrella. The smushed part doesn't have to be neat, just somewhat compact at the bottom. This forms the base of the flower.

8 **Bind with clear tape.** Hold the smushed base of the flower in one hand and wrap a piece of clear tape around it with the other. Since you are wrapping flat tape around a 3-D cone shape, you have to bend the clear tape any which way that works and holds. It will be covered in the end, so it can look messy. Just make it secure.

9 **Wrap with floral tape.** Wind floral tape around the base of the flower five times or so, covering up the clear tape. Then spiral the flo-ral tape down the wire to cover the stem as shown. (Actually, it's easier if you hold the tape in one hand and turn the flower with the other.) Cut and wind the end of the floral tape so it blends in.

10 **Open the flower.** This is the fun part, but do it slowly and gently to avoid tearing the petals. Take the outermost petal layer and gently pull it open, starting at one side and following it around. Do the same with the next layer in, and then the next. Sculpt and separate the layers until you are satisfied. The inner layers are harder to separate, but they naturally form a sort of pom-pom (especially if you chose to cut them with three slits), so you don't have to do as much to them. And if you make a little tear, it probably won't show, just adjust the petals to hide it.

COVER • BANDS

Homemade CD covers

We are lucky to live in an age where we can download music

in a trice. The era of the mixed tape has given way to the epoch

of the **mixed CD,** customized with love for a friend, sib, or

significant other. So why not put just as much care into the cover?

Play graphic designer and create a little piece of framed art.

MATERIALS

BLANK CD AND ITS CASE

WHITE OR COLORED
PRINTER PAPER, FOR
THE SONG LIST

MANILA FILE FOLDER
(or any other blank card stock)

PAPER EPHEMERA (old
magazines, photos, tickets,
pamphlets, postcards, gum
wrappers, etc.)

COLORED OR
SPECIALIZED PAPER
(optional)

STICKERS (optional)

TOOLS

COMPUTER WITH CD
BURNER

SCISSORS

GLUE STICK

DECORATIVE PAPER
EDGER (optional)

PERMANENT FELT-TIP
MARKER(S)

Getting ready

This is one of the projects you can make with what's already at home. Look through drawers and keep your eyes open in daily life for interesting paper bits you might otherwise toss—maps, playbills, junk mail, flyers for bands, invitations, and, of course, magazines. Anything with interesting text or pictures. Stay away from newspaper, since it will yellow. Stay away from thick cardboard. You want nothing fatter than a postcard.

How-to

1   **Burn CD.** Mix a variety of songs from favorite artists—Björk, Beastie Boys, Mel Tormé, whomever. Try a theme like lady rockers, or California artists, or the 7th track from all your favorite CDs. Or just DJ a good mix that flows. You can also burn a CD of digital photos to give as a gift.

2   **Make song list.** Type the song list into a new document on your computer. Use the print preview function to make sure that the block of text will not be larger than the 4¾-inch-square CD cover. Pick a fancy text style or go no-nonsense. Print the song list out on white or colored paper. You can also write the song list by hand. Handwriting adds a nice personal feel to a machine-made gift.

XOXO YOUR SONGS

1. Who Loves the Sun - The Velvet Underground
2. Soft Serve - Soul Coughing
3. Coming up Roses - Elliott Smith
4. Saturday Morning - Eels
5. Love My Way - The Psychedelic Furs
6. Here Comes Your Man - The Pixies
7. When the Roses Bloom Again - Laura Cantrell
8. Hooray for Tuesday - The Minders
9. Heart of Gold - Neil Young
10. Carried - Steadman
11. Don't Leave the Light on Baby - Belle & Sebastian
12. Carnation - The Jam
13. Tender (Cornelius Remix) - Blur
14. Greenman - XTC
15. I Don't Blame You - Cat Power
16. Wonderwall - Oasis
17. New Slang - The Shins
18. Tart - Elvis Costello
19. From Blown Speakers - The New Pornographers
20. Valentine's Day Is Over - Billy Bragg

with love xo

100% TRUE LOVE

Hannah & Robert
Prouts Neck, Maine
September 12, 2004

GETTING • SCRAPPY

If the CD is a gift, let your relationship to the giftee guide and inspire you. Use photos, tickets from a movie you saw together. Cut out words or pictures that illustrate inside jokes or pet names. There is definitely a scrapbooking element to this. If you have scrapbooking tools and techniques at the ready, use 'em!

3 **Cut out CD cover base.** Remove the premade CD cover booklet (if there is one) and trace it onto a manila file folder or other card stock, or simply measure a 4¾-inch square. Cut out the square. This will be the base on which you build your collage.

4 **Decorate CD cover base.** This is the fun part. Cut out text from magazines or junk mail. Cut out pictures from anywhere. If you like the texture or pattern of a picture—like an animal print coat from a fashion magazine—just cut out a square and use it as a mat for text or a mini background for another picture. Cut up photographs, candy wrappers, bits of ribbon, anything that's flat and appealing to you. Glue them into place with a glue stick. Build up layers. Add stickers. Follow a theme if you want, especially if the music has a theme.

5 **Cut out song list and attach to CD cover.** Take the paper with your song list and cut a square around the text (a decorative paper edger is

nice for this). The square can be any size smaller than (or equal to) the 4¾-inch-square cover base. Glue-stick the song list to the back of your CD cover collage. Embellish this side with stickers and cutouts, if you like.

6 Decorate the CD. Compact discs often float loose from their cases and land on the living room rug or under a car seat. Make the CD match the spirit of its cover so it doesn't get lost and forgotten. All the technical stuff is on the CD's underside. Keep that side clean. Label the CD top with permanent markers. Draw pictures or swirls. Decorate it with stickers. Just make sure the stickers are very, very flat so nothing can catch inside the CD player.

7 Place cover art in CD case. Open the CD case and slide your artwork under the nubs on the edges of the left side (the clear cover). The artwork faces out and the song list faces in. It's a ready-made frame for your collage. Put the CD in its niche. Make sure the case closes properly.

COVERING THE PAST

Album covers (the ancestors of CD covers) used to be the humble realm of the commercial artist or some guy in a suit at a record label. In 1967 pop artist (and former commercial artist) Andy Warhol designed a cover for Velvet Underground's debut album (Velvet Underground & Nico). It showed a big silk screen of a banana. That cover was revolutionary because it didn't portray the recording artists or even the music—it was its own piece of artwork. Warhol also designed the controversial Rolling Stones Sticky Fingers album cover (1971), which had a real working zipper on a picture of a man's tight jeans. Though he died in 1986, Warhol's covers are still among the most memorable.

SNACK-WRAPPER • WALLET

Plastic and foil food wrappers

can have an even longer shelf life when you sew them into handy

wallets. The result? Instant, functional pop art!

Perfect for carrying business cards, credit cards, bus cards, or

photo IDs. Make the whole thing in an hour or so.

MATERIALS

OILCLOTH SCRAP, AT LEAST 4 BY 3 INCHES *(available at fabric stores)*

SNACK WRAPPER, AT LEAST 4 BY 3 INCHES

COTTON EMBROIDERY FLOSS

PLASTIC REPORT COVER, CLEAR OR TINTED

24 INCHES BIAS TAPE *(the basic ½-inch wide single-fold kind)*

TOOLS

SCISSORS

PEN

HAND-SEWING NEEDLE *(large enough for embroidery floss)*

Getting ready

The challenge (and the fun) of this project is finding snack packaging you can cut and sew like fabric. Foil juice packs work. Reese's Pieces, Doritos, and PowerBar wrappers all work. Larger plastic bags that hold lots of bite-sized candies also make good wallets. Look for wrapping with big, bright logos and good graphics. Packages made of thicker plastic or with shiny foil on the inside tend to work best. You can test the packaging by poking through it with a needle (after you buy it, of course). If the material doesn't tear, you are on the right track. Look for imported food with cool packaging—like fruit candies and dried pea munchies. Ask friends to buy snack food for you when going overseas.

Oilcloth, the other main ingredient, is a wonderful, tough, flexible material that resists water and doesn't fray. You can make place mats, tote bags, and sunglasses cases with the stuff. Just sew it like any other fabric. Here oilcloth stands in for leather and lasts almost as long. If you find oilcloth in the scrap bin at your local fabric shop, that's pay dirt. Otherwise, buy a quarter yard, which is enough for at least fifteen wallets.

Last but not least, you'll need bias tape, so named because it's a ribbon of fabric cut on the bias—that is, slantwise across the fabric grain. Bias-cut fabric wraps nicely around curves, which is helpful when making the wallet corners.

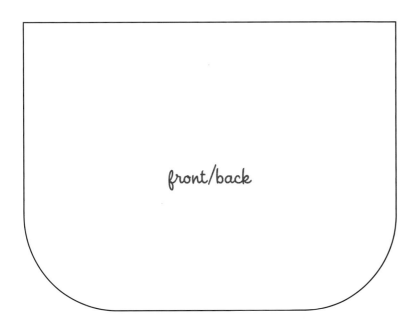

front/back

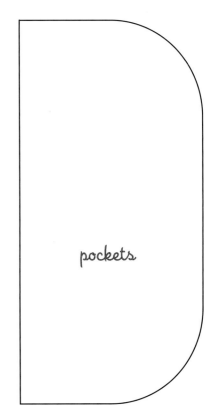

pockets

How-to

1 **Photocopy and cut out templates.** Label your templates ("front/back" and "pockets") so you don't get confused as you go.

2 **Trace and cut wallet back.** Trace the front/back template onto the oilcloth. If you are working with a floral or bold-patterned oilcloth, make sure to center the template over a part of the design that you like.

Steps 4 and 5: Sew front
and back together with a
running stitch. Sew a
second line of running
stitches to flatten
exposed seam allowance.

3 Trace and cut wallet front. Place the front/back template over your favorite part of the snack wrapper and trace the outline onto the wrapper. Make sure you have the template oriented properly. The curved corners will be the top edge of the wallet.

4 Sew front and back flaps together. Place the two flaps together, right sides facing out. Line up their straight bottom edges. Thread your needle with three to six strands of embroidery floss and sew the flaps together with a running stitch (see pages 116-117) about ⅓ inch away from the straight edge.

5 Open the front and back flaps and sew a second line of stitches. Pull the flaps open like a book. Lay the whole thing wrong side down, with the seam you just sewed sticking up (as if you were placing a book facedown on a table to hold the place). With your fingers, press the spine of the "book" to the snack-wrapper side so the oilcloth stays flat. If the underside of the snack wrapper peeps out from the spine, trim it back. Sew another line of running stitch in between the first seam and the spine edge, going through all the layers as shown.

WALLET + CALLING CARDS = EXCELLENT GIFT

Tuck a set of ten custom cards into a homemade wallet and remind your loved ones why they love you. Buy blank business cards at an office supply store and make personal calling cards using rubber stamps, words cut from magazines, or very neat handwriting. Your friend's name and a little decoration is plenty. He or she can write info on the back when giving cards out. They can also be name tags.

TIP

It's better to start sewing the bias tape on the oilcloth half, not the wrapper half, so that the bias tape ends will be hidden on the wallet back.

Step 7: Sew bias tape
around edges to hold
pocket in place and
create finished edging.

6 **Trace and cut wallet pocket flaps.**
Using the pocket template, trace two pockets
from the clear or tinted plastic report cover.

7 **Sew pockets into wallet with bias
tape edging.** Line up a pocket flap on the
inside back part of the wallet, matching curved edges
to curved edges. Fold one end of the bias tape in half
lengthwise for a few inches (you'll keep creasing it as
you go). Place the folded tape over the edge of the
wallet as shown at left so it makes a border that holds
everything together. Sew a running stitch through all
the layers, following the bias tape around the edges.

8 **Tuck under the bias tape end and
finish.** When your bias tape and stitching gets
all the way back to where you started, cut tape about
½ inch past where the ends meet. Tuck the raw end
under and keep sewing. Knot and cut off the thread on
the inside.

9 **Fold the whole thing in half.** The wallet
will be stiff at first and resist staying shut. But
after time in a pocket or purse, a permanent crease
will form.

INDEX

ACKNOWLEDGEMENTS

So many wonderful people helped make AlternaCrafts possible. I'd like to thank friends and family who donated materials (usually from their own drawers and closets)—Richard Vitkus (staunch craft supporter), Ann Allison, Jennifer Keller, Kenna Kay, Stan Hsue. Thank you to the talented artisans who helped me solve problems and tackle new areas of crafting—Dan Price, Jocelyn Worrall, Ryan McGinness, Lisa Vitkus. Thanks to Will Hines for computer help, and to Anna Jane Grossman for giving so much talent and time. Kathy Biscone was a demon with an iron. The AlternaCrafts models are sweet friends who jumped in to help—Josslyn Shapiro, Jacob Krupnick, Clay Weiner, Liz Sullivan, Vickie Lee, and her French bulldog Piglet. Thanks to Brian Kennedy who had both the patience and the eye to take all these gorgeous pictures, and to stylist Aaron Caramanis who created an inviting world in which the crafts could live. Thanks to Josie, Bayley, Devlin, and Max Claro-Resetar (all impressive crafters) for lending me their support and their mom. Thanks to their mom, Noël Claro, for helping me develop this book from the very start. There's no better partner in crafty crime than Noël. Her endless energy, patience, and ideas made AlternaCrafts possible—made the process a pleasure, made the results beautiful. Thanks to my editor, Melanie Falick, for taking a leap of faith and giving me the freedom to create my dream book. Thanks to my mom for reminding me, "Jessica, you are never so happy as when you are making stuff."